STONECOAST REVIEW

UNIVERSITY OF SOUTHERN MAINE

SUMMER 2018

ISSUE NO. 9

Dear *Stonecoast Review* readers,

We believe art should serve as a statement to the times in which we live. As the U.S. government cuts funding for both mental health institutions and women's rights organizations, it's no wonder both of these themes came to the surface of our Summer 2018 issue.

Our world, in the most important way, is carried in a woman's body. We open Issue #9 with the raw honesty of Stonecoast graduate Jenny O'Connell's "Still Life," as it invites the reader to consider what it means when we express the female form as art—a question continued with poems like Ann Howells' "October Sky" and Liz N. Clift's "I-90." Alexander Weinstein's "Unforseen Destinations" then takes us towards uncanny spaces, starting with the unbelievable tale of survival in Rita Anderson's original dramatic work, "Lightning Girl." From there, the line of the "real/unreal" evaporates entirely through the magical realism in both Jennifer Falkner's "Sometimes a Tree" and Theodora Goss' "In the Forest of Forgetting." All of these excellent narratives are punctuated by some truly evocative poetry and nonfiction essays.

Liminal spaces and the eclipse of mental illness serve as our secondary theme, approached tangentially through *original, never-before printed* stories from James Van Pelt and Rick Wilber. "Mambo No. M51" is a kaleidoscopic journey through a talented musician's galactic epiphany, while "Today is Today" shows us how even though reality's bubbles may change, compassion never does. We're also very excited to feature the hallucination-inducing poetry of UK-based poet **carrie carrie** for the first time in the States, and Brett Stout's artwork is a pulsing visual beacon throughout the prose, serving as a dynamic invitation with our striking cover and back-cover images.

We're also thrilled to publish voices from traditionally marginalized communities, including Dee Nathan's "Valid Identification" and graduating Stonecoast student Lee Kahrs' "Getting To Know You." Other Stonecoast appearances join us in the form of current student Devin Donovan's beautiful yet devastating "On the Eve of All Saint's Eve," through the awe-inspiring poetry of new alumna Orlan Roe Owen, and with the darkly humorous flash fiction "Cracked," by graduating student Carina Bissett.

As a final note, we thank everyone who sent us their work, including those who were not selected for this issue. We stand committed to providing customized feedback for at least half of all submissions, even if it's only a single sentence. Always remember that our art, though built from words instead of matter-based materials, is no different than any other artist's. Your story is not who *you* are. The pot is not the potter. For those who submitted for this issue but were not selected, we empathize with you. Out of more than five hundred submissions, *half* came from authors and poets who held MFAs or advanced degrees in English. When the prevalent themes for this issue began emerging, our volunteer staff searched diligently through the digital stacks—and we had to cut loose many enchanting stories. When an editor says a work is not the best "fit," sometimes that's truly all it means.

Each of us holds a flame burning at its own temperature. The stories, poetry, and artwork here were carefully crafted by our contributors, then forged through the kilns of our own hearts and minds. We hope your readings of them bring us all closer to understanding one another.

Yours,

Jess Flarity
Morgan Talty & Emily Bernhard

Masthead

EDITOR-IN-CHIEF: Jess Flarity

MANAGING EDITORS: Morgan Talty, Emily Bernhard

CREATIVE NONFICTION EDITOR: Jennifer Brooke

FICTION EDITORS: Cameron Gibson, Meredith MacEachern

POETRY EDITOR: Vanesa Pacheco

DRAMATIC WORKS EDITOR: Elliot Northlake

READERS: Allen Baldwin, Devin Donovan, Julie Cira, Kaitlin Nichols, Kate Kastelein, Kristin Leonard, Monica Jimenez, Nadja Maril, Pamela Stutch, Russell Wilson, S. Mack, Stephanie Loleng, t l elam, Tiffany Liang, Tyler Margid

COPY EDITORS: Monica Jimenez, Pam Joplin, Russell Wilson

LAYOUT DESIGNER: Monica Jimenez

WEB DESIGNER: Riley Flarity

ADVERTISING DESIGNER: Heather Meeks

SOCIAL MEDIA COORDINATOR: Vanesa Pacheco

TREASURER: Emily Bernhard

FOUNDING EDITOR: Alexandria Delcourt

FACULTY ADVISOR: Robin Talbot

STONECOAST REVIEW is published semiannually by students and alumni from the Stonecoast MFA in Creative Writing at the University of Southern Maine.
Inquiries should be directed to stonecoastreview@gmail.com.
Submission guidelines are online: stonecoastreview.org/submit

Find us on social media:
facebook.com/stonecoastreviewliteraryjournal
instagram.com/stonecoastreview
@stonecoastrev

Contents

Fiction

Poetry

Dramatic Work

Creative Nonfiction

Art

PHOTO BY JEFFREY ALFIER

Jenny O'Connell

Still Life

"...the only people for me are the mad ones, the ones who are mad to live, mad to talk, mad to be saved, desirous of everything at the same time, the ones who never yawn or say a commonplace thing, but burn, burn, burn like fabulous yellow roman candles exploding like spiders across the stars..."

Jack Kerouac

The first day, I wear my hair down so it might cover more. The professor gives me a pillow and politely asks if I would twist my body here, lean back into the light, bend just slightly at the knee. Hold it.

The light undresses me.

"Don't be afraid to get messy," he tells the class.

No, I think, posturing my body, which I woke up an hour early this morning to shave and pluck and paint.

"Let her take up the whole page," the professor tells the class.

No, NO, I think, sucking in my stomach.

I try to be thinner.

The students in their skinny jeans ripped intentionally at the knees, the students wearing mismatched socks, the students swimming in their hooded sweatshirts, they regard me. Hunched over their easels, they fill the room with scraping charcoal and the sound of paper. I watch their eyebrows, furrowed with concentration, as I pass through the meat grinders of their imaginations and out onto canvas. Sometimes they draw my body better than it looks. Other times, they draw it worse. This one makes my jawline look very flattering. That one makes me fat. Another one makes me blue. *Sorry,* they say when they see me looking; true artists, always the first to forsake their work. I pretend it's all just a bad yoga class. I hold the poses for so long I forget to suck in.

I am a University Art Model. It's a part-time job I picked up for fifteen dollars an hour. I always add the "University" bit because it makes the idea of taking my clothes off in front of a roomful of strangers and letting them draw me sound more legitimate. Right now, I'm wondering if this is worth the forty-five dollars I'll earn today. Seventeen minutes go by. I've never been so aware of the clock. Someone sneezes. "Bless you," I say, becoming human again.

The professor guides me into a different pose. Sit up, back straight, left leg folded over right, spine twisting toward the left. I'm not sure I like his voice, gentle but distinctly male, telling my body what to do. I definitely don't like my body following directions without question. My left foot falls asleep.

"Pretend she's a landscape," the professor says. "Bodies are intimidating. Landscapes are not."

I want to tell him about the most intimidating landscape I know. Grizzly bear country, Alaska, maybe, or the Cordillera Blanca mountain range in Peru. How I walked into the Alaskan backcountry with a tin can, a pebble, and a screw to ward off bears. How I ran from Andean bulls at sixteen thousand feet. I want to tell him about the thirty nights I slept outside in negative-fourteen-degree Adirondack winter. In the landscapes I travel, bodies are the least intimidating thing. But to say this would betray my purpose. I came here to learn how to sit still. I came here to learn how to stay.

CB ᔑ◦-᎒ᔐꙄ

What sets a life in motion?

For me, it was the sound of tires hitting black ice on Interstate 88. More like the absence of sound, really. When tires hit black ice you expect to hear screeching, but you hear nothing. In the absence of sound there was only my white Toyota RAV4 flipping over the guardrail and rolling one, two, three times into the median.

It was January 2009, my first winter out of college, and I was driving the barren stretch of upstate New York highway from my boyfriend Jesse's place in Corning to my parents' house in Albany. When the car stopped rolling I sat very still, suspended at an odd angle by my seatbelt. I craned my neck to see. Outside, the world was white-glazed grass. The world was ice. Freezing rain fell like ticker tape on the passenger door window, now strangely above my head. My phone lay open near my feet.

A rush of cold air as the passenger door opened. Three wet faces appeared, spotty in the darkness above me. I stared blankly up at them and waited for someone to tell me what to do.

"C'mon," said a man's voice. I unbuckled my seatbelt and slumped onto the driver's side window. Found my feet and stood. The sound of my boots on the plate glass confused me. "Missed the river by this much," I heard someone whisper. "Jesus." One hundred yards up the road, a river bent through a seventy-foot ravine.

Three pairs of hands grabbed under my arms and hoisted me out into the ice-crusted night. One man climbed back into the wreck for my backpack. I stood shivering until someone took me by the shoulders and ushered me toward the road, where a woman wrapped me in a blanket and sat me in her car with the heat on full blast. As the warmth spread through my limbs, I expected to feel something, *anything*—nausea, headache, whiplash, fear—but nothing came. The woman said she was watching me for signs of shock, so I gave her a weak smile and tried to appear calm.

The state trooper pulled up behind us, lighting the car mirrors up in electric red and blue. I thanked the woman, collected my backpack, and climbed into the patrol car. The trooper asked how fast I had been going. "I'm going to pretend I didn't hear that," he said when I told him. He looked down at his electronic note-taker and shook his head. "Do you know how lucky you are?" he said.

I nodded, and peered through the ice now gathering on his window. That was when I saw my dad.

He was striding toward me in the dark, white hair a beacon, hunching his shoulders against the rain. My dad, the Navy veteran. The bravest man I know. My dad, whom I'd only seen cry twice—when he read the names engraved on the Vietnam War memorial in D.C., and when our dog died. My dad, who answers the phone when I call with bells in his voice. My dad, who sends texts in capital letters:

HI JEN, IT'S DAD
I LOVE YOU
LOVE,
DAD

My family's love is messy and unadorned and raw. We wear it plain on our faces. I don't remember my dad's face that night. I only remember the way he stood outside the patrol car and hugged me—strong, soft, and breathless, like he'd just had the wind knocked out of him. Which was how I knew he was afraid.

∞

The second time I model at the university, I've just driven five and a half hours from my parents' place in New York. I haven't showered in two days, I haven't shaved in a week. I wear my hair up. The professor is a soft-spoken woman who gives very light direction. I get to choose my poses. The students are freshmen and sophomores, and they are shy. Their eyes dart at me and then quickly away. It seems like they are trying to draw my body from memory.

"Use your imagination where the drawing stops. Draw what you can't see," says the professor. One of the students is playing music on his phone, a movie score battle soundtrack. Another student is sketching with a pencil on a paper plate. The room is cold. My stomach growls loudly enough for everyone to hear. I hold ten short poses for thirty seconds each, and then lie still and listen to the clock, which seems to be ticking in slow motion.

Recent studies have found that when something threatens your life, a walnut-size area of the brain called the amygdala goes into overdrive. The amygdala hijacks resources from the rest of the brain, forcing attention to the situation at hand, slowing perception.

I remember everything about the moment my Toyota hit black ice. The gleam of the guardrail, lit up in high definition by headlight beams. The fishtailing car; the lurch of the steering wheel. The metallic crunch as the passenger side door struck the rail, flipping me. My cell phone dropping from between my cheek and shoulder. My friend Steph's voice, tinny and frantic, on the floor. Upside down, right side up, upside down, right side up, I floated.

I wonder what else happened in my brain that night.

When Jesse heard about the crash, he almost missed his plane to Australia, where he was moving after college to study for a year as an Outward Bound instructor. For the next six months we communicated by letters and the occasional phone call, until I used the money from my wrecked car to buy a plane ticket. We stood ankle deep in mud in the Australian rainforest, surrounded by the mating calls of bell birds. Jesse took my face in his hands as if preparing to hold it for a long time. "It's hard, to be in love with someone who's in love with the world," he said. I thought of the time we went to Chinatown, the way he'd looked at me when I'd tried to fit a crab into my water bottle to set free at sea. *I wanted to give it a second chance,* I'd said.

Jesse dropped his hands.

CB ॐ ॐ ৪0

"Adventure" comes from the Latin *adventurus,* a thing about to happen, and *advenire,* to arrive. In the decade following the crash, I became a person who lived somewhere in between the two, uncertain whether I was running toward or away. Seven countries, four continents. If there was a mountain, I wanted to be on it. If there was a language, I wanted to speak it. "Hurricane Jenny" is what my family called me. I became a person who slept in too many airports, who cried when the sunset was too orange, or when the night janitor in Terminal B whistled a melody so haunting it roused the sparrows, who resettled on the television monitors. On more than one occasion I crashed my bike looking at the stars, which were one of the few things that centered me. I'd lay there in the road and stare up at Orion with hot tears running into my hair, begging him to show me home.

I lived my twenties as an outdoor guide and led expeditions with students—backpacking, rock climbing, whitewater rafting, sea kayaking, International exchange. After they went home, I'd release myself into the landscape: lose my way on a peak at altitude after dark, get into a cab with a stranger, attempt a river crossing alone. I don't know why I did it, only that it had something to do with the way my heart felt when I got myself into trouble and back out again. I'd always had a propensity for adventure, but now it was amplified by the fact of my mortality. Over and over, I acted out my escape. There is a side of risk only felt in the body. Primitive. Instinctual. Suspended between safety and the ultimate failure of death, I could fly.

Jesse wasn't afraid of death. He could die today, he said, and never regret it.

I was mad to live.

CB ॐ ॐ ৪0

Tuck right arm beneath neck, bend right leg, left leg straight, head turned to the side. I'm sure my stomach is pooching more than anyone would think attractive. My thighs, goose-pimpled in the cold winter light, feel colossal. I hold the pose for longer than I think reasonable. I hold the pose for longer than I think possible. My right arm falls asleep. We take three breaks, and each time the professor asks I return to the same position. I become less interested in my thoughts, which I suppose, in its own way, is a form of grace.

Maybe this is what staying is: the body.

The breath rising in my chest. This precise cold. The way my dad leans back in his chair and closes his eyes to listen to what love sounds like the way Gershwin hears it. The presence to notice; to know this will not be forever.

I hear it on the glass studio skylight: outside, freezing rain is beginning to fall.

When I remember I'm going to die someday, I burn, burn, burn, afraid to be dull. I pour myself a glass of wine before noon on Sunday. I call up whomever I'm dating and say, "I want your breath on my cheek, *now*." I run my hands over their skin to feel the soft warmth of it. Try to memorize their faces. I take my time. Sometimes, I just hold their body against mine to feel their aliveness pulsing beneath, my mouth pressing into their shoulder, hungry for love.

Cups are being washed, brushes rinsed. The students are finished. I wrap myself in flannel and walk around to each of their paintings. One woman is still working. With blackened hands she moves her charcoal across the paper, drawing where the drawing stops. *Sorry,* she says. I smile at her and watch her lines, the way they join, the smudge and texture. On her page, my body is alive. I realize I have forgotten what a body is. These days, my dad, the bravest man I know, sits at the top of the stairs and struggles to tie his shoes. "No man in my family has ever made it over seventy," he often says, and now I am the one who's afraid. When I hug him, I hold on a little too long. Some nights I stay awake just to hear him breathing in the other room. A body is a miracle.

I dress in an adjacent classroom, grateful for my hunger and the ache in my feet. My body is not a landscape. The light is fading and sleet is coming down hard now. In the studio, the students are discussing their art. As I pull on my coat, I write a letter in my head, address it to my future lovers, to all the insecure parts of me. *Missed the river by this much,* it begins.

I open the door and walk out into the rain.

PHOTO BY MARIA GREEN

carrie carrie

Chasing Information

The real is shimmering in and out and in
(and in and in like a collision course
blurred through collision, in and never out,
 just blend and blend and blend and entropy
or its opposite), and I catch my breath
as though it were a Grab and Go sandwich,
wedged into a stopgap of present in
an ellipsis that never stops. THE END
repeated again and again again.
And I try to understand everything.
 Follow the leads everywhere. Down the dark
allies where I will wish I'd never walked.
 Brand EVERYTHING on my well done brain meat
as though to cure influence anxiety
and reconcile the micro with Macro,
all in all, but my brain was not designed
for stream-of chaos-phantasmagoria
and I regret my strange experiments
and pin them down attached to epithets
to demagic them, repeating the task,
Information box in lines of squares—
streaming into new eternities—
of having Fallen into infospheres
influenced not by Pure Chance but People,
 swimming in strange hells of other minds—
but choice, sometimes/somehow more frightening,
kicks away the dice—but they still roll
and decisions can't *always*—go wrong
after the button-push—heartbeats—
 of the perforation on the line—
between past and present too observed—
to saunter over the lines and the squares.

Earworms

In a feedback loop of my own making made out of notes of words and not of words,
a wild goose chase with origami geese whose honking is, somehow, more startling than
tetrahydrocannibinol—made mindmusic like angels on answerphone, all sound no fury,
and mouthvolcanoes until
I am a samovar, self—boiled, a Swan of Tuolena swum so deep that I've un—am—ed myself,
and murdered sleep, insomnia—paralysed, an a—machine that no—one can turn off or
powercut, a Turing machine infested with earworms.

Ponds

I used to cross roads from ponds of filth-black,
Scum-mold-green—not to glimpse their contents.

I used to cross roads from graveyards for that
same reason—not to scratch their surface.
I dreamed of a monstrous paddling pool,
swarmed with writhing things with scales and teeth(ing).
The same sensation when I walked through c(o)unt-
ry roadside grass and suddenly smelled DEATH,
and I remembered a book describing
that same Nausea. Now I understood.
The same thing when I swam too far out—
a sea-b(u)oy's chain fronded with strange sea-plants.
The same thing when I watch the floor puls(e)-
ate, too tired not to see it.

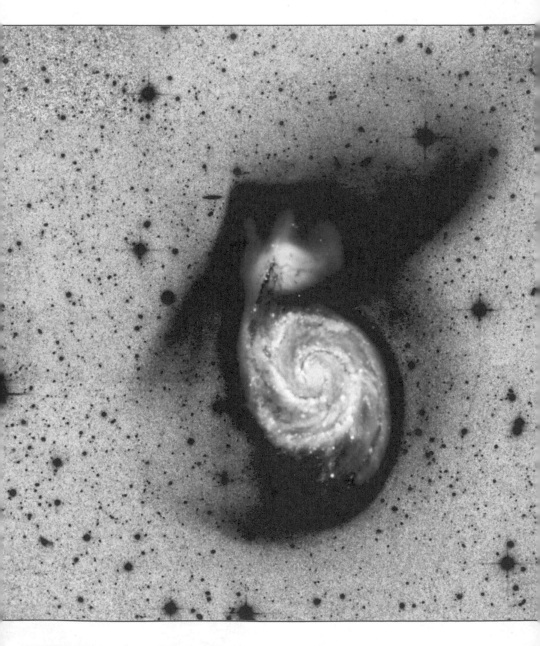

PHOTO BY GIUSEPPE DONATIELLO

James Van Pelt

Mambo No. M51

Emma Sophia lounged in a cast chair by the offstage food table, eating a celery stick and eyeing the backup dancers languidly. "I'm thinking of changing my name to 'S,'" she said. "The great ones only had one name: Cher, Madonna, Sade, Rihanna."

"The letter, or are you going to spell it out?" I sat in the canvas-backed chair next to her that read ASSISTANT DIRECTOR, but I was really one of the post-production CGI guys. Music videos aren't anything until we get hold of them.

"Just the letter's curve. It's about the shape." She closed her eyes and sighed. "Shapes, patterns and rhythms. The universe is an information paradise, if you have an eating-lion mind." She draped one leg over the chair's wooden arm. Everything she wore was black: knee-high boots, nylons with fashionable tears, leather shorts, and an armless, leotard top, also torn, like a tiger had taken a swipe at her midriff. A black biker's jacket completed her look, covered with steel studs and zippers, matching steel-studded black gloves. White hair washed over her shoulders.

Emma Sophia had been voted "sexiest pop artist of the year" for the last two years in a row. She also could have been voted nuttiest, if they had such a category.

Men and women dancers moved into position on the Armageddon set, a series of stages surrounded by industrial pipes and rusted machinery, while the lighting technicians rotated through the colors hidden behind the props: violet, red, turquoise, peach, and a hellfire orange. Metal clanged against metal. The set smelled of water, baby oil, sweat, and electricity.

"Get in the mood! Get in the mood!" yelled the choreographer, who began clapping her hands. "It's a rave at the apocalypse, dance against chaos. Everything's desperate. Everything's foreplay. One last orgasm before the end!"

In their torn outfits, the dancers looked like they'd just come from a catwalk knife fight at an exclusive fashion show. Lots of unexpected skin and toned legs.

I asked, "Are you in this bit?"

"They'll call me when they're ready. Is the room done?" She leaned toward me, a breathtaking movement, her jade-jeweled eyes fixing mine.

"Yes, it's ready."

"Sound system? You programmed my mix?"

I nodded.

"Good." She put in a pair of earbuds and thumbed her music player to life, leaving me to my own thoughts.

℘⸎⸎℘

Two weeks ago, when I first met her, she asked me if I wanted to listen to her personal song collection. She had a top-notch setup, with expensive, noise-suppressing buds custom fit for her ears, although they did okay in mine. I took them from her, trying not to tremble. I'm post-production, for crying out loud. I'm not the kind of guy who hobnobs with Emma Sophia. I don't know how she knew who I was, but she had asked for me.

Static came through her earbuds.

"It's broken," I said, popping one out.

"Keep listening."

A heavy snapping, like porcelain clicking against an anvil, and a rushing fuzz.

"Still static," I said. "Is that what I'm supposed to hear?"

"That's the Crab Nebula. Did you know that space makes music? You can find thousands of radio telescope recordings. You can even hear it live. I've got my top ten here." She held the screen where I could see her playlist: M51, Jupiter, Orion, Xi-hydrae, the Pillars of Creation. "Have you ever listened to something a hundred times in a row?"

"No... but I've watched the same video footage more times than I'd like to count."

"It's sort of like that—like standing in front of a painting every day. At first it's all the obvious stuff. Color. Composition. You get it in ten seconds. But when you come back again and again, you see the picture underneath. Once I spent a week looking at just one corner of Bruegel's *Fall of Icarus*."

"What did you see?"

She didn't answer, and after a while I thought she hadn't heard the question.

"Immolation," she finally said.

CR ∴ ⅌ BO

The actual assistant director had told me, "She's damaged. Runaway OCD, or something."

He laughed, an ugly snort.

"She loses time. Missed a concert once. Everyone was in a panic. 'Where's Emma Sophia? Where's Emma Sophia?' And when they found her, she was plopped down in front of a TV staring at the interference pattern between television stations. Took them an hour to snap her out of it. Some kind of self-induced coma—prima donna whack job."

CR ∴ ⅌ BO

It was hard to ignore what the director said when Emma described the special room she wanted me to build for her.

"High-def video screens all the way around," she said. We were standing in her dressing room on the set, a small space stripped bare. That day she wore running shoes, jeans, and a Led Zeppelin T-shirt. She still blazed like a laser.

"So, four big screens," I said, puzzled. She didn't need a CGI expert for that. A call to any electronics store could get whatever she wanted installed.

"No, wall to wall, one continuous screen and the same on the floors and ceiling. Seamless. Everywhere I look should be screen, and then I want them so that they all show a single image, like 'The Veldt.'"

I raised my eyebrows.

"It's a story about a kid's nursery with the same arrangement," she said. "You don't know it? You'll need Plexiglass on the floor to protect the screens, but it has to be totally transparent, like aquarium glass." After explaining the story she said, "At the end, the lions *eat*," which was the title of her platinum album from last year. I didn't know what it had to do with this conversation, though, or if it connected to her "eating-lion" mind.

21

I jotted notes and tallied an approximate cost. "That's going to be expensive. What do you want to display?"

She laughed, preoccupied, with her hands behind her back, like she was imagining it already. "I'll send you the images. You'll need to do your CGI magic on them."

"A forest, or something?" I said.

"It'll be my holodeck."

"Um, like Star Trek?"

"Or something. The new song—my song for the video—it's a mambo. Have you heard it?"

I shook my head.

"Rock and roll mambo. Listen to some mambo before we talk again. I'd like this set up as soon as possible."

So, I listened to mambo while I ordered the equipment. It started in Cuba, you know. Perez Prado. Beny More. It was a dance craze. But Emma Sophia's rock and roll mambo didn't sound much like it. Every once in a while a string of notes reminded me of the stuff I'd been listening to, and if I turned down the guitars and synthesizers, the beat hit right. Her version was a distant cousin, all techno and over-dubbed magic.

At my apartment, I tried the fuzz between television station bit, like she did. My sixty-inch screen hissed and popped and scattered gray randomness at me, but I didn't see what she saw. I couldn't put myself into her "eating-lion" mind.

I'd never done a total immersion video room, but the software to handle it was straightforward. Not something an ordinary laptop could render, of course, but not outrageous either. I put tiny, almost invisible speakers in the room's corners, massive woofers behind the screens, and installed a couple of projectors on swivel-heads that synced the image with the user's movements. I liked the forest idea. If she took a step, a nearby tree would slide in front of one farther away, giving her the illusion of a three-dimensional world.

Instead of a forest, however, she gave me pictures of galaxy M51. The first picture showed its entire spiral shape hooked to another smaller galaxy called NGC 5195. If I turned the picture on its side, it looked like a momma apostrophe towing a baby apostrophe. She gave me other pictures too, showing details, the glowing gases between the stars, nova remnants, dust, swirling shapes. To create the image I had to assign distance values to the individual elements, creating a snarl of databases and equations. After a few days, all I could think of were star coordinates, brightness, color.

CB ও--ও ৪০

Emma Sophia closed her eyes, turned up the volume. I could hear clicks and hissing, even over the noise from the set. Makeup interns spritzed water and baby oil on the dancers to look like sweat. Not that they needed it.

"First positions! First positions!" yelled the director. Then the music slammed through the speakers. Dancers moved to the rhythm, pulsing in unison. Their routine was pure arousal: writhing, rubbing, slippery slick bodies moving against each other in sync to the music. Overhead sprinklers came on, drenching them. Water droplets flew from fingertips and hair.

I checked my monitor for placement and light on the green-screened dancers off to the side. Post production went easier if the lighting was right the first time. I needed their feet in every shot for the apocalypse effect we'd drop behind them later, and I constantly had to check that the camera crew shot the dancers in their entirety. Directors seem to think that their mistakes can be fixed in post, but the process is way easier if the footage is right to begin with.

An assistant choreographer tapped Emma Sophia on the shoulder. She didn't respond at first, lost in her galaxy music. He shook her deferentially. She still didn't move. Her eyes were closed, but I could see them twitching, like dream sleep. Then she unfolded from the chair, sinuously, and took her spot on the stage. Strange, bell-like sounds came from her ear buds on the seat where she'd dropped them.

I know musicians, some "real" ones, who think that Emma Sophia was just the pop flavor of the year, that she wasn't serious or even artistic in any sense. But they never watched her dance. She took the front and center position, fists up, elbows tight to her ribs, then she caught the beat in her legs and torso, and the dancers behind her mirrored her moves, like shadows or puppets attached to her strings, moving to her mutated mambo done with electric guitars and synthesizers and percussion machines. She lip-synced the lyrics.

"No! No! No!" she said when the song ended. "The bridge is all wrong, and half of you are sleepwalking."

I wondered how she decided that, since, for most of the dance, the troupe had been behind her. She stalked among the dancers, who stepped aside.

Emma Sophia showed them what she wanted. "When I do this," she spun to one side and then did a complicated shuffle with her feet, "you need to be here." She showed them the move. The choreographer made changes to her notes.

The director spluttered from behind the camera, "We'll have continuity problems. Half of that's already shot. You can't change the routine without redoing everything."

Emma Sophia stopped mid-dance step and glared into the darkness where the director sat. Water dripped in the background. Plink, plink, plink. But no one moved. No one spoke. I found myself gripping the chair's arms.

The director's voice, sounding resigned, said, "Or we can reshoot."

Emma Sophia nodded, then went through the routine again, moving dancers from spot to spot.

Somebody said, not loud enough to reach the stage, "Forty thousand dollars a day, and we're three days behind."

Those folks who didn't think Emma Sophia was serious didn't see her work that day. Multiple costume changes. They soaked the dancers over and over, including Emma Sophia. She insisted they do the same twenty second segment dozens of times. "Not good. Not sharp," she'd say. They ended the day when a male dancer collapsed. As the shoot's doctor examined him, he said, "Just give me a minute. I'll be fine." He could barely wave his hand. "Don't replace me."

Emma returned to the chair next to me, toweling her hair dry. "A good dance is like sex," she said. "It's not over until everyone is spent." Her eyes sparkled with anticipation. I couldn't tell that she'd been dancing all day. "Can I see the room now?"

Suddenly, I was nervous.

The room was at the end of a long hallway. Fortunately, the outside walls were open to the studio, as running the power and video cables through a building's walls would have been a nightmare. As we approached, I slowed. "This could cause sensory overload," I said. "Are you sure that you should go in? Will you be safe?"

She put her hand on my arm. "That's sweet. They aren't seizures, you know."

"Sorry. I didn't mean to get personal."

We stopped at the door, and I realized how small Emma Sophia was. The top of her head didn't reach my chin. In her videos, she seemed larger, dominating, almost a superhero or a goddess, a dancing pop deity.

I showed her the remote, a modified game controller.

"That's power on-off, and this controls sound. The main function, though, is the joystick. You use it to move through the galaxy like you're flying a spaceship. You'll be maneuvering through three dimensions, and it can get disorienting. If you mash the accelerator, you cover about ten light years in a second. You'd blast through the entire galaxy in an hour at that rate, or you can slow down, explore, hover over a sun." I laughed as I handed the control to her. "You can even go into a sun, but it gets bright in here if you do."

She opened the door. I'd set the displays to show a robin-egg blue for a default, but I found even the resting color made me a bit dizzy. The Plexiglass held us two inches above the floor screens, but there was no way to judge distance. When the door closed, a rectangular hole in the robin egg blue universe disappeared as the displays seemed to meld into the color on either side. Blue abyss loomed below and above. Limitless blue everywhere.

Emma Sophia said, "My God," the blue reflecting off her cheeks and eyes. She rotated slowly, taking it in.

"Let's do it." She pressed the start button on the control.

The walls darkened, and I waited for the program to boot. Emma Sophia breathed softly beside me. In the darkness, I reached for her hand, but I pulled back before we touched.

"We'll begin a hundred light years away, from the Earth side of M51," I said.

The galaxy brightened on the wall opposite from the door, stretching far above our heads and below our feet, a giant spiral swirl of violet gasses, maroon veins, and thousands of glittering suns. Stars faded into existence around us—other planetariums were cheap replications compared to this.

Slowly, she accelerated us toward M51. Stars slid by overhead and underfoot. I stepped back to regain my balance and swallowed against the vertigo.

"Sound," she said. "I need a sound track."

"Volume and track selections on the side. Stellar recordings and your own stuff. You can do mixes too."

A leaden bell throbbed in the room, then a high hiss backed by a rhythmic tang, like a hammer tapping a bed spring. Her radio telescope star sounds.

I needed to hold onto something solid, but other than Emma Sophia, there was nothing to grab, so I sat cross-legged on the Plexiglass, swaying in vertigo's grip. She didn't seem bothered, though. At first she just navigated toward the galaxy's center, like an arrow plunging toward the bull's-eye, but soon she swooped from one side to the other, diving down so stars flew from wall to floor to wall to ceiling. She turned the sound volume higher and higher until the bass thrummed in my chest, then she aimed for a single star that swelled into a hundred-yard-wide, fiery globe. I could imagine the heat baking against my face beyond Emma Sophia's silhouette in a searing, pop star eclipse. A radio telescope rendered corona crackled and spat through the hidden speakers as great gas plumes shot from the surface.

Emma Sophia was just beginning.

She laughed, a beautiful sound, before plunging us into the star itself. I clenched my eyes against the brightness, and then we were through, the star receding behind.

"It's the mambo," she shouted above the rush of celestial music. Behind the stars' whistles and tinny heart throbs and hornet buzzes, her mambo rose, and she began to dance with her galaxy.

I've watched all of Emma Sophia's videos, the ones when she was a teen phenom, the older ones when she decided to throw off her innocent image, the scandalous ones, the sacrilegious ones, the award winners and the bombs. I knew her entire catalog, but I'd never seen her dance for herself—dancing in a galactic core, dancing for the stars, dancing for her music.

And the universe spun for me, too. My inner ear didn't help.

Were *we* spinning, or had she started the stars on a slow rotation? Which direction was up? I felt for the Plexiglass, but I couldn't touch it. I was floating. I was falling. Weightless in the illusion of perfectly rendered stars, and in the midst of it, Emma Sophia, dancing, undulating, responding to the rhythms and being the rhythms. Over the mambo and stellar sounds she laughed again, a delightful cascade of human joy. Passing by me, starlight glowing off her face, she touched my shoulder as she moved, a momentary pressure. Then the stars rushed by. We were plunging or rising or crossing, and diamond lights stampeded past. But for how long? How long? Time compressed or expanded, a lot of it maybe, almost as if we were traveling near the speed of light, as if we had accelerated ourselves to relativistic speed, but I had no sense. Had she danced for ten minutes, or ten hours?

She moved like a native creature, an outer space denizen who belonged in the abysses between the great suns.

We passed a ringed planet, like Saturn, and then an irregularly shaped rock, asteroid pitted and deeply shadowed. A star whose leaping plasma jets turned the room orange, then mauve, brushed by, buzzing and crackling like cooking bacon or a long wash of wave retreating from a stony beach.

I wanted to close my eyes against the dizziness and the hallucinatory depths, but I couldn't take my gaze off Emma Sophia. She no longer danced, now facing the approaching stars as if she'd taken the boat's prow. Her back was to me, her posture unnaturally rigid. The mambo slammed through the speakers, and I stared and stared.

"Emma Sophia," I cried to her. "Emma Sophia!" But she didn't move, her feet apart, her hands resting, relaxed on her hips.

Slowly, I braced myself until I was standing. Stars crept by, underfoot and overhead. In the distance, stars appeared to be heading straight toward us until they finally drifted to one side or the other, above and below. We were falling through M51, unanchored in time and place.

She didn't react when I touched her arm, when I gently took the control from her hand. The stars winked out, and the screens resumed their default blue. Up close, Emma Sophia's eyes seemed shaped from glistening green marble, but they didn't react when I blocked her vision. They didn't move when I shook her shoulder. She was gone, really gone.

How long had we been in the room before I stopped the display? Were her security people looking for her yet? If they weren't, they would be. We didn't have long together before they would come, and I knew that wherever she had gone in her head was a long way away. Would she come back? What was it like there?

"I love your sound," I told her.

I twitched the display control. The light faded and we stood among the stars. I turned the hisses and crackles up and faced M51's glowing center, a million transcendent pinpricks in the dark fabric. If I stared in just the right way—if I listened with my eating-lion mind—maybe I could join her. Maybe we could rush through the galaxy together, dancing, looking immolation in the face and becoming its shape and pattern and rhythm at last.

ART BY BRETT STOUT

PHOTO BY MARIA GREEN

Ann Howells

October Sky

Grackles turn in flight,

a sorcerer's black cape,

fold, fold again.

Dusk bends to smooth

her indigo stockings.

Her pink lipstick

smears the horizon.

Liz N. Clift

I-90

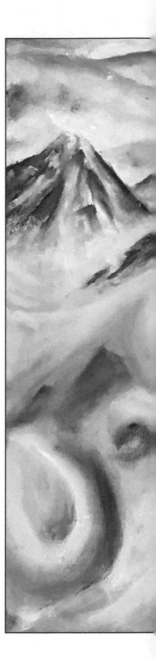

Ghosts unspool into trees
glittered by this winter fog, and
who doesn't imagine getting lost
with Montana, the way she kicks
up her mountains
of skirts, the way her laughter whips
snow across ranches. We could wait
out winter in her valleys until
wildflowers spread like carpets, until birds
take up song to woo the grasshoppers.
Montana will take us from plains
to peaks, and we'll find ourselves sitting
at the headwaters of the Missouri,
watch the water rolling
sleepily by, floes forming, the way
spring comes like gunshots, the
water angry and roiling, or she'll
invite us into the hills above Missoula
or onto her glaciers and damn anyone
who calls her frigid—ever—she'll
break us, again and again, teach
us to learn lessons from bison
which once huddled here, coats
crusted, breath clouding, feet stamping.
Everything is only fleeting, and Montana
will let her cold settle into our bones
so we know what it means to be warm
and well-fucked.
Montana's ground is restless,
these mountains new, her heartbeat
the hot springs, her breath the seasons.
We should learn to steady our breath
this way, inhale, exhale, exalt.

ART BY CARL ERICKSON

Dee Nathan

Valid Identification

The new birth certificate arrived a month ago. My heart raced as I texted Lance for permission to open the package. I wanted to rip it apart and make sure "they got it right" but was afraid to damage the contents. I delicately pulled out three copies of the document—and there it clearly stated that on May 12, 1994, I gave birth to a boy named Lance Miller. I sat alone on our front porch steps as tears escaped my eyes and rolled down my cheeks. I wasn't sad—but I was definitely emotional.

I had helped Lance extensively through the arduous process of a name and gender change. Although Lance wanted it badly, he wasn't up to the effort of getting through all the red tape required to have his name and gender officially represent who he is. I became his facilitator and cheerleader.

I was giddy at every juncture of the process: the judge's stamped declaration of his new name, the new Social Security card, the doctor's letter affirming his gender, the affidavits and official documents and all the waiting periods in between. I gave Lance a huge high-five when the DMV finally submitted his documents for a new driver's license.

But the birth certificate was different. It was the final step in his self-declaration of who he is.

Coming out as a lesbian at the age of forty-two puts me in the category of being late with my own self-declaration. I didn't deny my sexuality prior to then, I just didn¹t follow the hints of it throughout my adolescence and young adulthood. I adopted social norms and didn't question conventional rules. But that was the 1970s and people seemed less self-aware and less "out" than they did in the 1990s. My first marriage had been to a man. I had given birth to four children. I had thought my second child was my daughter—there weren't a lot of clues that I should think otherwise.

When I divorced and fell in love with a woman, our family dynamic shifted.

Krista had a young son, and she and I blended our families. Her son and my youngest (genetically born a boy) found solace in each other's company and formed a tight bond; my two girls and Lance (then still presenting as a girl) went into adolescent hell. We were a thunderstorm of a family: liberal, open-minded, tumultuous, and imperfect. We muddled through years of everyone struggling to find their special place. As a family of seven, we appeared as two parents, two boys and three girls. Yet, more than a decade later, Lance's decision that he was trapped within the wrong gender wasn't a revelation.

Lance had struggled with an eating disorder for many years, while also battling anxiety and depression, all exacerbated by an ever-present sense of body dysphoria. After much therapy and deep introspection, Lance came to the conclusion that the dysphoria could never abate if some significant changes were not made. Being in the body of a female was increasingly ill-fitting, and although Lance didn't feel a hundred percent male, he knew with all his soul that he wasn't meant to be a girl. So Krista and I embarked on the medical journey with Lance, securing the appropriate doctors who would help him transition his body from something alien to something comfortable.

Having been raised by two socially and politically liberal mothers with careers in the arts, our kids are nothing short of progressive millennials. So it was not surprising that they embraced Lance with support, openness, and humor. Our family didn't spend a lot of time mourning the loss of our sister, our daughter. We were too busy welcoming Lance.

Accumulated suitcases and boxes of Lance's former clothing were opened, and his sisters joyfully embraced the additions to their own wardrobes. It was a rite of passage; Lance was purging the outer trappings of his burdensome past, relieved that his sisters embraced what he no longer could. The girls, in turn, celebrated Lance's evolution—no longer a sister, now their third brother. I am the closest in clothing and shoe size to the girl Lance had been, so I inherited what didn't fit his sisters. When I wear these clothes, I reflect on both the person he used to be and the identity he has since bravely claimed.

And while I'm proud of our kids for letting their hearts lead the way, they are not perfect by any means. On our last family vacation a few months ago, we had booked three hotel rooms for the seven of us. Two rooms were to be shared amongst the five kids. Lance's siblings all came to us behind his back. It seems none of them were willing to have Lance room with them. Not the boys' room, not the girls' room. I was speechless.

The boys declared discomfort with having their former sister see them in any state of nakedness. The girls, though they had grown up sharing rooms with Lance, respected his now-male identity and therefore did not want to be naked with their new brother.

I reminded them that Lance is still the same person they grew up with, albeit more self-realized and slightly different physically. But neither set of kids could make peace with sharing their intimate space with him.

I was sad—and frankly—disappointed in all of them.

I believed we had all adjusted so well. But I have found there is usually a breaking point at which family members pause and take in how gender change affects them personally. For me, it is Lance's emerging beard, on my former daughter's face, that is making it difficult.

And I suspect it won't be the final hurdle.

PHOTO BY BRETT STOUT

ART BY BRETT STOUT

Alexander Weinstein

Unforeseen Destinations

from The Lost Traveler's Tour Guide

Previously published in Exit 7. *Reprinted with author's permission.*

The City of Berholtz

Though filled with everything a traveler could desire—sunny skies, afternoon strolls, and coffee roasters serving cappuccinos—Berholtz proves incredibly difficult to leave. Attempting to check out from your hotel, you'll find yourself trapped behind an old man inquiring about a shoe store; a group of tourists barricades the doorway with their luggage; the airport taxi is driven by a man with no clue about the city; and as you watch the airport growing smaller, your cab driver will ask if *you* know how to get to the terminal. And just when things have begun to look brighter—the cab has made a U-turn, and the airport is getting closer—you'll encounter standstill traffic a mile from Departures. At this point, the most frantic travelers will open their cab door and flee. Through the stalled traffic they go, suitcase in hand, crossing cattle pastures, until they reach the barbed wire fence preventing them from reaching the tarmac.

Because of the days, weeks, months, and years of waiting that a seasoned traveler will accumulate in Berholtz, it's worth noting that waiting is one of the common destinations we'll all frequent. Full of melancholy and frustration, waiting is a preparation for the other destinations of waiting we're bound to visit: the weeks of emptiness after our children have left for college and we await their return; the months waiting for a new relationship; the years spent waiting for a promotion; waiting to be noticed; waiting for a sandwich; waiting for the pain to end and the pleasure to begin; waiting in concourses, bus terminals, train stations, and hotel lobbies; and between this, an interminable span of time waiting for our kids to be ready or the shower to be free. In fact, your guidebook writers often wonder if waiting isn't the destination we've all been waiting for, teeming with life, waiting for us to arrive.

For those who find themselves standing in the cow pastures of Berholtz, we offer this one consolation: there's a mysterious providence given to those willing to embrace the city's delays. As you listen to the gate agent inform you that your flight has been indefinitely cancelled and there are no flights home, consider that connections are missed every day. Picnics are ruined by rain, dream jobs are given to other applicants, departing busses huff exhaust as we run toward them, and the loves of our lives pose for wedding photos with strangers. And while most of us gripe and complain about layovers, there is a rare type of traveler who, upon seeing the stalled traffic of Berholtz, grows more at ease.

It's true, your guidebook writers have encountered very few such travelers, but in the brief encounters we've had, we can report this: they're much happier than we are. What's more, they tell stories of magnificent restaurants discovered on the night of their delay, of a job opportunity offered by a stranger at the airport, or of a sunset more beautiful than any they'd ever seen. They sat and watched it at an outdoor café with another stranded passenger. Come, let me introduce you to my husband, they say, you'll never believe how we met.

The Art Institute of Zanir

When people speak of Zanir, they're usually referring to the Art Institute, not the city itself, which is comprised of drab, Bauhaus-era apartment buildings and concrete playgrounds. These buildings, once the apex of architecture, have suffered the fate of their nearsighted architects, becoming the boxy, windowless dwellings where citizens of Zanir measure out their lives in weekends. Each day, the inhabitants tramp down stairwells and ride the decrepit monorail to the nearby factories, where they stamp documents and sell two colors of carpeting. There's a munitions factory, where men in pale blue jumpsuits assemble weapons, and when the whistle blows, they carry their lunch pails home in the darkness. Indeed, when describing Zanir, few are speaking of this city, for which no tourist would ever book a vacation.

Zanir is better known for its Art Institute, which was founded by a philanthropist who'd amassed an enormous fortune manufacturing bathroom tiles. Behind the darkened curtains of his office, Victor Bethog spent most of his life on the phone with people whom he had no love for. His voice never rung out in song, his body never moved in dance, and his walls contained no art, only framed sales awards. One evening, during a business trip abroad, he encountered a young girl playing a fiddle on a street corner. Her music echoed within him, and he suddenly envisioned his life as a long and pointless march toward death, filled only by financial figures and two-toned tiling. And so he returned to Zanir with its grim skyline, and devoted his fortune to transforming Zanir into a *City of Art*.

Many wondered why the city would want such a thing. Apart from the crayons one gave children at local restaurants, there was little art in Zanir. Citizens shook their heads as they watched the construction from their windows, and they joked about the school's demise during cigarette breaks. And yet, among those who mocked the plan, there were others who recalled a book they'd once hoped to write, how they sung while showering, or danced in their kitchens when no one was watching, and, that spring, they broke forth from their homes to enroll at the Institute.

Bethog funded the students for as long as they wished to stay. He provided them with workspace and materials free of charge, and he purchased nearby apartment buildings to serve as residencies, covering the artists' rent in exchange for gallery openings, concerts, poetry readings, and theatrical performances. And soon, more artists emerged—dancers, painters, writers, actors—and entire city blocks transformed into divisions of labor which included *The Rooftop Painters, The Car Dealership Poets,* and *The Grocery Store Orchestra.* Those who chose to stay at their old jobs stared at the celebration from their fluorescent-lit offices and wondered what they were doing with their lives. They wrote to the Institute, seeking admission, and within the year, bosses removed their ties, departed through lobby doors, and joined the city's marching bands.

It's hard to say where the school's center is anymore. The streets are filled with murals and musicians, its citizens are filmmakers, painters, and playwrights. Yet one senses when one has exited the campus. Out there, at the edges of the city, you can still find the colorless buildings where men and women return from their factory jobs in the evening. Their living rooms are lit with the glow of the news, and they close their blinds and turn up their televisions. It's too difficult, they say, to look out the windows and see the city with all its colored lights, to see all that dancing.

The Theater of Unfulfilled Dreams

Have you ever wished to sit at a bakery with a new lover, to have your hair stroked as you fall asleep, or simply to hear the words *I love you* whispered in the dark? If so, the Theater of Unfulfilled Dreams will perform all your unmet desires for the price of a ticket.

Here, at Khlax's oldest theater, a troupe of actors came together to perform *Plays of Longing* in the last years of the millennium. An actress, who'd never said goodbye to her father, delivered her final soliloquy on stage, while an actor, too poor to travel, visited distant streets beneath the lights. But though the performances were transformative for actors, critics called the plays a form of solipsistic therapy, and audiences faded. Eventually, the actors closed the theater's doors to the public and retreated inside, where they continued to perform their productions for the next twenty years.

Why then, on a spring day, two decades later, did the theater reopen? Perhaps the decision was due to its younger actors, who longed for an audience, or maybe it was the older actors who'd grown tired of the familiarity of their longings. The opinion surfaced that it was time for the group to turn their focus outward again. Why not help the inhabitants of Khlax fulfill their unrequited dreams, the actors asked. And, suddenly, passersby noticed a new sign on the marquee, and an illuminated box office wherein a woman stood ready to sell tickets and listen to the citizens' deepest needs.

Soon, many came seeking inclusion in the plays the theater produced: lonesome men who wanted to be surrounded by actors for a birthday party; a widower who wished to celebrate her golden anniversary; some wished to hold a beloved's hand as they walked beneath a stand of trees; or to sit at a café and play chess with a friend; and many wanted nothing more than to hear their parents' praise. They'd sit beneath the theater lights and share the news of their latest business venture, and the actors would lean forward, take the audience member's hands in their own, and say, "We're very proud of you."

Since its reopening, the theater has lines of eager theatergoers. Tourists arrive with their own requests and we buy our tickets, watching the lights brighten as actors emerge from the wings, urging us to step onto the stage. When we sit in the audience, we watch the others—the fathers and mothers, teachers and janitors, neighbors and strangers—and are surprised by the familiarity of their stories. Leaving the theater, we find that the world is populated with people whose longings are miraculously similar to our own. Perhaps, we think, it always was.

PHOTO BY JEFFREY ALFIER

Rita Anderson

Lightning Girl

This original dramatic work is a fictional account based on the 1971 Lansa 508 airplane accident, in which Juliane Koepcke was the sole survivor.

Characters:

Juliane Koepcke: Biologist, grew up in Peruvian rainforest.

Mother: Maria Koepcke, Juliane's mother, well-known German zoologist.

Ensemble (#1 & #2): Shapeshifters, a part of the jungle.

Woodcutter: The one who finds Juliane in the forest.

Radio (Voiceover): Actual quotes from reports surrounding the event.

Time/Setting:

Shifts, suggested. Surreal. [Inspired by true story.]

Stage:

Pitch dark.

Only the sound of a soft drip breaks through the darkness.

As lights come up, the trickling gets louder, more insistent: this isn't just any trickle, but a lifesaving runnel of the Amazon River in the Peruvian rainforest. [The creek will be Juliane's way out of the jungle, where she's trapped, now in 1971.] Huge ferns and elephant-ear-sized leaves represent the rainforest's fertile flora. [Is an airplane wing, a seat, the fuselage etc. of a downed plane hidden under the lush vegetation?]

Dressed in a miniskirt and one sandal, Juliane is asleep on the jungle floor.

Ensemble and Mother emerge from the greenery to laugh and dance. It wakes Juliane, and she joins their childlike dance.

All: *Ring around the Rosie.*
A pocketful of posies...

Juliane breaks out of the circle dance to assume an adult stance, perhaps many years in the future. Another time. Another place—

The present.

Mother: When are you going back to Peru, Juliane?

Ensemble: *Nothing can be reversed.*

Juliane: This summer, Mama. When my teaching term ends. Like always.

Mother: To Peru, yes, but—

Juliane: —*and* to Panguana, Mama!

Mother: —our research station!

Juliane: Of course our research station, Mama. (laughs) What's gotten into you?

Mother: Dearest Panguana...

Juliane: (reassuringly) Yes, Mama. I love it too.

Mother: What's become of it?

Ensemble: *Nothing can be annulled.*

Juliane: (laughs, touching Mother's arm) The nature preserve is thriving, Mama!

Mother: *It's a preserve now?* (beat) Ah, good! Good.

Juliane: And I've told you that a thousand times.

Beat.

Mother: You live such a full, beautiful life, Juliane!

Juliane: You really should come see Panguana for yourself again. You and Daddy.

Mother: Hans is too old to travel.

Juliane: (on cell phone) Then look! Here's what Panguana looks like in [use current year] 2018. It's on Google maps now!

> Mother doesn't look. Instead, she joins Ensemble again. They play another childlike game and, holding hands, they form a line and call out to Juliane.

Ensemble: *Red Rover!*
Red Rover!
Let JU-LI-AN-AH come over!

> A slow roll of thunder stops her from joining them, and the game breaks up. [Thunder acts like a transition, a jump in the time/space continuum.]

> Juliane turns to Mother. It's 1997.

Juliane: I got the job, Mama!

Ensemble #1: *May 1997.*

Ensemble #2: *Dear Dr. Juliane Koepcke—*

Ensemble #1: *—we'd like you to head up our Bavarian State Collection —*

Ensemble #2: *—of Zoology.* (beat) *In Munich.*

Mother: You're moving *again*?

Juliane: Top in my field.

Mother: Like your father and I were, yes.

Juliane: Aren't you proud of me?

Mother: I want you to be happy, Juliane.

> Sounds of thunder and animals of the rainforest.

> While speaking, Mother distances herself from Juliane.

Mother: Happy, Juliane. Are you *happy*?

> Juliane watches as Ensemble #1, a jaguar now, circles them hungrily.

> Mother, unaffected by the predator, speaks here as if giving a lecture.

Mother: Exhibit A. *Otorongo.* Tupi-guarani for jaguar, the "beast."

Juliane: And, Mama. (beat) I'm getting married!

Thunder. Another shift, another rift.

Mother: (listens to correct her daughter) But you've been married for twenty years, darling.

Juliane: Of course! That's right! What was I thinking?

> They share a laugh.

Juliane: But where's my ring? (freaks out) I can't find my wedding ring!

> As she searches for it, more thunder. Time shifts to 2011.

> Juliane, excited, has Ensemble hand Mother official documents and a plaque.

Mother: What's this?

Juliane: It's about Panguana.

Mother: Oh, my precious birds!

Ensemble #1: *It's about the research station—*

Juliane: —that is named after your birds, Mama, yes!

Ensemble #2: *Those ten kilometers are now a private conservation area.*

> Mother is so proud.

Juliane: Officially, now! Protected.

Mother: It's a dream come true! A dream.

Juliane: And, Mother? I'm going back, you know.

Mother: So you said, this summer—

Juliane: To Peru, yes. But I meant—

Mother: —like always!

Juliane: —back to the crash . . . well, 2011 *is* the fortieth anniversary.

> Beat.

Mother: Is this about that director?

Juliane: He wants to make a movie about me.

Mother: I hope your father and I have taught you the importance of water, Juliane.

Juliane: Well, back to the *site*—

Mother: A small creek leads to a big one. Leads to a river. Leads to life.

Juliane: —if we can find it. You know how the jungle likes to swallow things.

Mother: (detaches again, a lecture) The cana brave is a *giant* reed which covers the mouth—

Juliane: (nods) The mouth of the creek we followed out of the green hell of the jungle. Where we, later, showed the rescue team the way back to the crash . . .

Mother distances herself from Juliane again.

She assumes the formality of a professor lecturing.

Mother: I am Maria Koepcke. My specialty is the birds of Peru.

Juliane: (laughing, to audience) Mother was always bringing birds home. Birds that had been injured or shot—

Mother: (smiling, to Juliana) —and that we brought back to health!

Juliane: (to audience) For a while, tinamous were her favorite, and mother had a real knack for this. Not once did a chick she was raising die!

Mother: (distancing, back to formal lecture) The tinamous, *Eudromia elegans*, are a shy, secretive family of bird found in Central and South America.

While Mother gives her bird lecture, Ensemble hunt Juliane, predator and prey.

Mother: One of the most ancient living groups of bird, tinamous have small wings and prefer to walk or run away from predators and other danger, but, when they've exhausted all other evasion techniques, they *can* fly, albeit poorly.

Juliane: Mama?

Mother: Their plumage doesn't usually differ between sexes, but some females are brighter, and tinamous females are in charge. They have to defend their turf.

Juliane: *Mother*? Where do you keep *going*?

Mother: Luckily, tinamous young are *precocial* and can run almost as soon as they hatch. Scientists believe they are self-sufficient in twenty days.

Juliane: Mother! It seems that every time I try to talk to you about the crash, you disappear.

    Sound of thunder.

Ensemble #2: *Charred pieces of carpet.*

Juliane: Jungle as far as the eye can see...

Ensemble #1: *The strands of which have now grown into the ground.*

Ensemble #2: *The jungle keeps what it can find.*

Mother: (louder, now, to stay in her thoughts, safe) Panguana—

Ensemble #2: *Metal frame of a suitcase. Locked.*

Mother: —our ecological station—

Ensemble: *The emergency door.*

Mother: —was a mile big! With a Lapuna tree—

Juliane: —with its tall, fanning crown—

Mother: —dead center. It was easy to spot!

Ensemble #1: *Fragments.*

Ensemble #2: *So densely strewn.*

Mother: In the densest—

Juliane: —virgin—

Mother: —rainforest. With—

Ensemble #1: *An instrument panel.*

Ensemble #2: *With a length of cables.*

Ensemble: *Still attached.*

Juliane: Our mission was to catalogue the massive biodiversity at Panguana. We counted five hundred different trees!

Ensemble #1: *A debris field so thick that the rescue team.*

Mother: —four hundred species of ants. And—

Ensemble #2: *Could barely walk. A coin purse.*

Mother: —three hundred fifty bird species!

Ensemble #1: *A tray. The handle of a spoon.*

Juliane: Two hundred eighty butterflies—

Ensemble #2: *The heel of a woman's shoe.*

Juliane: —and fifty-two species of bat—

Mother: —which you once lived inside of a rotted tree *for a year* in order to study, Juliane!

>   Sound of thunder and Juliane, Mother return to that 2011 conversation, an argument.

Juliane: And I know you don't like it, but I've agreed to go with him, that director.

Mother: *Juliane?!*

Juliane: Back to the *site*.

Mother: No.

Juliane: He even booked me the *same* seat. By the window.

>   Upset, Mother detaches again.

Mother: I study birds, so I hate to fly. (beat) I find it totally unnatural that a bird made of metal takes off into the air. It's not normal, I tell you.

Juliane: Can you believe? The *same* seat! So, once again, I'll be—

All: —Passenger 19F.

>   Sound of a giant thunderstorm, and, as it wages, Ensemble forces Mother and Juliane into a frantic circle dance, spinning faster, faster.

All: *Ring around the Rosie.*
A pocketful of posies.
Ashes, ashes—

Sound of a lightning strike. Flash of bright light across the stage.

Ensemble: *—We all. Fall—*

Mother: (an actual quote) This is the end!

All: *—Down!*

All break away and out from the circle, spinning crazily about, then "landing," one by one, in odd positions, dangerous angles.

Silence.

Then, the sound of the creek.

Finally, the sounds of rescue crews.

Radio (V.O.): After lightning hit Lansa Flight 508, ninety-two Passengers disappeared into the Peruvian jungle without a trace.

Mother slowly stands, gets her bearings.

Ensemble #1: (slowly standing) *We did not leave the airplane.*

Ensemble #2: (slowly stands) *The airplane left us.*

Ensemble and Mother re-enact that busy day at the airport, December 24, 1971.

Juliane's still "asleep" in the spot she was in at the play's start: her landing position after the crash.

Ensemble #1: *Due to increased storms over the mountains, all flights have been cancelled.*

All grumble.

Ensemble #1: *There is, however, one final flight out, Lansa 508.*

Ensemble #2: *Is this a joke? Didn't know Lansa had any planes left.*

Ensemble #1: *They have one. And this is the last flight. You want it or not?*

Mother and Ensemble #2 fight for the flight—and they both get tickets.

Mother: (an actual quote) We ninety-two are the lucky ones—

Ensemble #2: *—who will make it home for Christmas!*

They high five.

Radio (V.O.): The most extensive search in Peruvian aviation history has yielded nothing...

Ensemble #1 is a Woodcutter now.

Woodcutter: *I was out chopping trees in the rainforest and heard a loud bang. Like an explosion. I told the rescue team. But no one believed me.*

Mother moves to where Juliane sleeps.

Mother: Get up.

> Juliane gets up—but only in her dreams. She steps away from Mother, who still stares down where Juliane's body is still "asleep" on the ground.

> She waves her hand in Mother's face. Nothing.

Juliane: For three days, I dreamt in a fog. I was alone, walking down strange streets I'd never been to. Not another soul in sight, I stared into shop windows. But all the mannequins had broken faces. Heads smashed. Disfigured.

Mother: Can't stay here, Juliane. We have to find a way out. To the Amazon—

Ensemble: *The river that lies, that pretends.*

Mother: Juliane, wake up! This instant!

Juliane: And the clouds? I'd never seen anything like them.

Mother: Look for running water. And listen for the calls of the crested chicken—they nest by rivers! And rivers are where you'll find a village.

Juliane: Clouds like huge, moving creatures. Turbulent. Terrifying.

Mother: Bond with the jungle, Juliane. Bond! We're afraid only of things we don't understand.

Ensemble #2: *Stingrays in the murky shallows.*

Mother: You can do this, Juliane. Panguana is *home*. Remember your training!

Juliane moves frantically. (Is she waking?).

Juliane: Then, all of a sudden, I'm . . . I'm *outside* the plane. Suspended in midair.

Ensemble #1: *But falling fast.* (pointing) *From two miles up—*

Juliane: —I fell.

Mother: Human beings tend to destroy everything that frightens them.

Ensemble #2: *Crocodiles.*

Mother: Wake. Up!

Juliane: I sailed through the air with my row of seats. Then I spiraled, face down. Seatbelt squeezing me. I can't breathe.

She faints.

Mother runs over, shakes her awake.

Ensemble pulls back the vines, greenery that hides the wreckage, exposing it.

Mother: Can you walk, Juliane?

Sounds of rainforest fauna—everything oozes, slithers.

Ensemble #1: *Piranha.*

Juliane: Lost my sandal, Mama.

Mother: You have to move.

Juliane: I'm hungry.

Ensemble #2: *Food found at the crash site: a bag of candy—*

Mother: Get that tree trunk, those large leaves.

Ensemble #1: *—a Christmas cake, soaked in mud—*

Juliane: We'll cover ourselves.

Mother: Just until morning. (beat) Get up!

Ensemble #2: *—severe concussion. A broken collarbone—*

Juliane and Mother walk through the jungle.

Ensemble #1: —*eyes so bloodshot*—

Ensemble #2: —*they thought you were a forest demon.*

Mother: Don't stop, Juliane! The jungle takes no prisoners.

Ensemble: *But after ten days, the search for survivors is abandoned.*

Juliane: Eleven days. I lapsed into a kind of trance.

Ensemble #2: *Minor injuries. Considering*—

Ensemble #1: —*she fell from the sky.*

Juliane: Haha, look! Mama! There it is. The cana brave!

Mother falls behind.

Mother: Advance, Juliane. (beat) Just keep going.

Juliane: It's the reed that covers the mouth of the creek we followed out of here!

Sad, Mother stops, shaking her head.

Mother: No. (beat) That *you* followed, honey. *Out*. Get out.

Juliane runs to a purse and picks it up.

Juliane: And! Your purse. Mama, I found your purse!

Juliane tries to give her mother the purse, but Mother holds out her hand to stop Juliane.

Mother: No! You can't.

Juliane: I can't what? It's your purse. Take back your purse.

Mother: I can't.

Juliane: What do you mean, you can't? Why can't you?

Juliane tries once more to return the purse, but Mother moves farther back into the jungle.

Juliane: *Mommy*! Just take your purse—and let's go. You're scaring me.

Sound of thunder.

Ensemble turns their backs, and, holding hands like a line of paper dolls, they resume the child's game, but the tone is changed. The game is no longer playful, and, when they call Mother, it's more of a summons.

Ensemble: *Red Rover!*
        Red Rover!
        Let MA-REE-AH come over!

Solemnly, Mother joins ensemble; backs still turned, they let her in the line and all hold hands. From Mother's purse, Juliane pulls out a wedding ring.

Juliane: But? What is my wedding ring doing inside your purse? *Mama?*

Juliane holds up the ring and approaches Mother in Ensemble line, their backs still turned away. No response.

She puts the ring back in the purse, and then touches her face, considers her clothes.

Juliane: I . . . I just finished high school. It's still 1971? But, I don't understand. (beat as she remembers, correctly, now) My prom! It's why we were late getting home. To father in Peru. To Panguana. *Mother?* Why won't you answer me? Look at me. Please, Mama. I'm begging you.

Mother and Ensemble turn.

They hold skeleton masks (or clear masks with no expression) over their faces.

Juliane: I don't understand.

Mother: I will never leave the jungle, Juliane.

Juliane: Nonsense! The way out is there. Right there. Come with me!

Mother: I don't get out, my love.

Juliane: But—

Mother: But you need to go, Juliane—my *cheerful one.* Go!

As Mother disappears back into the greenery, the sound of the Amazon River is almost deafening. Juliane breaks out of the forest canopy and into the light.

Ensemble acts as Woodcutters who discover Juliane when she emerges.

Woodcutter: *What?! Is that?*

Juliane: Are you real?

She falls to her knees in exhaustion, sadness, relief.

Ensemble puts a blanket around her, and they lead her off in exit.

Radio (V.O): (actual quote) Today, on Epiphany—January 6, 1971—after twelve days in the Amazon, seventeen-year-old Juliane Koepcke, the sole survivor of LANSA Flight 508, walked out of the jungle. It's nothing short of a miracle . . .

PHOTO BY MARIA GREEN

ART BY CARL ERICKSON

Christine Holmstrom

I Love You, Nightstalker

The notorious killers attracted the most admirers. Men like Richard Ramirez, the Nightstalker. He'd been convicted of thirteen murders, multiple counts of sodomy, rape, and fellatio. Said that killing sexually aroused him.

Despite, or perhaps because of all that, the Nightstalker attracted groupies, women looking for a relationship with an infamous rapist-murderer.

It's not like I hadn't done a bunch of stupid things myself—such as having lousy, guilt-ridden sex with a friend's husband and then being too embarrassed to hang out with her again. I'd stuck with boyfriends who'd pushed me, slapped me, choked me out, and a husband who'd chased me around the house bellowing like an angry bull. But marrying a serial killer? It was unthinkable.

I'd gotten plenty close to notorious criminals just by working at San Quentin. When I started as a new correctional officer—prison guard—I'd been surprised by the gore groupies and fangirls. In an assignment as the evening institutional phone operator, I'd fielded telephone calls for Charles Manson, the sixties cult leader who'd sent his followers on a bloody rampage, murdering pregnant Hollywood starlet Sharon Tate and several others in a wealthy L.A. neighborhood.

"Is Charlie there? We want to speak to Charlie," the high-pitched voice on the other end of the phone had asked. Giggles bubbled through the speaker—schoolgirls looking for entertainment. Beside me, an oldies radio station was playing Elvis Presley's "Love Me Tender."

"Prisoners aren't allowed to receive calls. You can write him if you want."

I'd stared at the black phone console, wondering how old the callers were. Twelve, maybe thirteen. Did they think that the swastika Manson had carved into his flesh above the third eye—the chakra of enlightenment—was a charming bit of body art?

"We can't talk to Charlie? Bummer. Well, do you have any other cute campers we can talk to?" More giggles.

Those girls probably called on a dare. Or out of boredom.

But others were serious.

They visited, even married condemned inmates despite no chance of a conjugal visit. A hug and a kiss on entering and leaving the visiting room was all that was permitted, unless a couple could sneak into the ladies' room or behind the vending machines for a quickie. How did condemned inmates like the Nightstalker become minor celebrities? What was the attraction? Why did women write, visit—even long to marry—an avowed Satanist, a man who'd gouged out one woman's eyes and had sex with the fresh corpse of an elderly victim?

I thought I'd had my head up my ass when it came to romantic choices. There was Roger, my first college sweetheart, whose love notes and sprigs of flowering oleander deposited in my dorm mail slot never made up for his jealousy or complete disinterest in my sexual satisfaction. Or junior college dropout Gary—the lover who'd provided cascading orgasms but was nearly evicted for failure to pay rent, and sometimes had to ask me for bus fare. Then alcoholic James, twenty years my senior, who couldn't say he loved me despite telling his bar buddies that he wanted to marry me. Or philandering Stephen, whom I did marry, but soon divorced because of his wandering ways and fierce temper. Who was I to look down on these women's compulsion to hook up with condemned prisoners?

After a few years as an officer, I'd been promoted to correctional counselor, spending hours mesmerized by the crime summaries and evidence photos in condemned men's files. I found them disgusting, yet fascinating. Still, I was glad for the sturdy iron bars that separated the killers from me when I walked the tiers, and for the correctional officers who stood guard over inmates during interviews or casework sessions.

One morning, as I'd been waiting in the Adjustment Center (AC) sally port, the secure controlled entry to San Quentin's infamous lockup unit, a cop entered with Richard Ramirez, the Nightstalker. The AC gave me the creeps—especially the bullet-pocked walls from the '72 takeover and slaughter of staff and inmates. I could almost see the bloodied bodies stacked like discarded furniture on the indifferent concrete floor.

The weather had been warm, perfect for a short-sleeved floral summer dress and strappy black sandals. Ramirez stared—his eyes laser-focused on my feet, examining the arterial-red polish on my toenails.

My skin rose in bumps, as if I'd been pushed alive into one of those refrigerated compartments at the morgue. I'd pressed my stack of inmate files against my chest like protective armor. The escorting officer, his broad hands gripping the prisoner's waist chains, seemed oblivious to Ramirez's odd obsession, how he visually caressed each of my carefully pedicured toes.

I'd almost said, "What, necrophilia isn't enough? You've got a foot fetish too?" Instead, I'd averted my eyes. The Nightstalker continued to stare—Satan's icy claws penetrating my flesh.

Later, inside the AC office, the phone blared. A woman wanted to write to one of the condemned prisoners.

"I'm married with three kids," she'd said. "I'm wondering—should I use my home address or get a post office box?"

You should get your head examined, lady.

I'd hesitated, chewed my lip. "It sounds like you're worried about your family's safety."

Did her husband know? And why did she want to correspond with a serial killer?

I sucked in a steadying breath and asked.

"I'm curious," she'd said. "I want to understand, to help. Maybe if he'd had a better childhood, he wouldn't have become a killer."

Biting my lower lip, I'd stifled the urge to berate her, to wise her up.

I'd heard it all, listened to the callers who believed in the condemned man's innocence, the ones who got their kicks writing to Charlie Manson or Tool Box Killer Lawrence Bittaker, the lonely hearts types with some odd mass-murderer fetish, people with rescuer fantasies, the church ladies out to save souls.

I figured a few men on death row were likely innocent—victims of bad cops, lousy lawyers, racism. But what about the condemned who were proud of their misdeeds, the ones where evidence of guilt was indisputable?

Who were these women who signed up for the serial killer fan club, who married unrepentant killers? I'd had my share of lousy relationships, made bad choices—including taking the prison guard job at San Quentin. What was *my* motivation?

You could say I had an unhealthy interest in evildoers. But I wasn't marching down the aisle with any of them. I got my rocks off reading their files, trying to figure out what turned a kid into a killer. Often, there was little information about a condemned man's childhood and upbringing. And even when there was abuse or neglect, it didn't explain why that particular person became a heartless murderer. Ramirez was raised in a devout Catholic family, the youngest of eleven children. No mention of abuse. As a teen, he fell under the influence of an older cousin, a Green Beret who'd served in 'Nam, a man who regaled Richard with tales of torturing and mutilating Vietnamese women, providing Polaroid proof of his crimes. The two smoked dope, discussed Satanism. Later, the man murdered his wife. Young Richard was there, saw it all. Was that the final piece in the puzzle, the thing that prompted Ramirez's enlistment in Beelzebub's army—what led him to embark on a murderous spree?

After the Nightstalker's arrest, groupies wrote him love letters; many wanted to marry the Satanist. Fans attended the trial, some clad in black robes. A forty-one-year-old virgin and journalist named Doreen Lioy fell in love with his mug shot, which she insisted showed his vulnerability.

How many times had I projected admirable qualities on a potential lover or spouse—despite evidence to the contrary? Excused bad behavior because of a boyfriend's childhood trauma—his mother's abandonment or suicide? At times I could still feel James's calloused construction-worker hands on my throat, remember pleading, "God, please stop," while he snarled, "You don't even believe in God."

Ramirez found Doreen's virginity "attractive." They met and married, breaking the hearts of the Nightstalker's many female admirers.

"He's kind, he's funny, he's charming," Doreen said in an interview. "I think he's really a great person. He's my best friend; he's my buddy." She even planned to commit suicide if Ramirez was executed. Her family disowned her.

Mental health experts have several theories about the reasons women marry serial killers. Some see the man as powerful, a protector—an alpha male. Others want to nurture the little boy that the killer once was. A few seek status and recognition through their infamous spouse. Many, I suspect, have a misguided sexual attraction to killers. Like the woman who said, "One thing that interests me a lot about serial killers, psychopaths, and sociopaths is how they deviate from the norm and don't really care. Violence is just exciting. It's a bit like Russian roulette—my turn could be soon and he could kill me. Spice things up a bit. Conventional stuff is boring."

I understood the desire for excitement. After listening to a radio show about the most unusual or daring places women had had sexual encounters, I'd straddled my boyfriend as we were speeding across the Bay Bridge after a night in the city. How long were his eyes closed when he came? How close were we to a fatal crash? I didn't think about the danger, only the thrill. I suppose it was the danger that created the thrill.

Perhaps I was more like those serial killer fans than I cared to admit. But I definitely wasn't planning on marrying any of them. I was just a voyeur. That was enough for me.

Helen Waters

Toileting

My boyfriend and I aren't doing well as a couple. We've reached a really long plateau. And we've said, "The right answer—the right thing to do—will become clear to us."

There is a lot of politeness.

This morning is a good example: He was getting ready to leave for work and I didn't have to rush out, so I sat down on the toilet with *The New Yorker* that came in the mail yesterday. But he started talking to me from the kitchen, so I opened the door just a little bit to hear him better. And he was being so open and vulnerable about his feelings concerning a situation he's been dealing with in his band. And I thought about what he was saying and responded, attempting steps toward reconciliation, still trying to make our partnership work, making myself care. And he kept talking, but walked to the other end of the apartment, so I had to open the door wider, and I leaned out from the toilet a little to hear him, but I couldn't, so I said, "I can't hear you," and he walked all the way back. And so I was sitting with the door open, *The New Yorker* on my lap, kind of trying not to poop so I could keep talking to him.

There is a picture of me somewhere—I'm ten years old, naked, sitting on the toilet with a book on my lap. I've blocked out who took the picture. Probably my mean-at-the-time older stepsister. But I know why it was taken. Around that time I started to get sick when I ate. And I was constipated a lot. That's why the picture was taken.

Because it was so notable to my family how long I'd have to spend in the bathroom. My best friend at the time told people at school that I was constipated. Fourth grade was hard. I saw a lot of doctors. One lady pediatrician even put a gloved finger up my butt. So many tests. The last thing I had to do was poop into a plastic cup that my mom took to a lab. And it was discovered that I had an amoeba. And in case you don't know, you can only get an amoeba by swallowing fecal matter. By swallowing poop. And it was determined that I got mine swallowing lake water at the state park. A week of antibiotics and that was it.

But I'm thirty now, and I'm still weird about poop.

I had to say this morning, "I'm sorry to interrupt, but I'm really uncomfortable talking like this."

And it broke something, I think. I can't really remember much but his disappointed tone and that he thought we were past the point in our relationship where things like that mattered.

I don't really know what happened—except that I got to close the door.

PHOTO BY TRAVIS VOLK

Genevieve DeGuzman

Mandala

A bear mother in the forest wears fish skin for paws. When she wakes one day in bleak winter, maybe as she feels herself opening, giving birth to her cubs on a December morning, she will remember an old throbbing rooted in the keratin scars that carry her. She will remember those distant dreams of wood smoke and blood over coals. Of silver dashed scales. Of tidal froth hypnotized to the moon. She will remember how something was wrested from the water and pinned on. Pinafore memory brief as lupine blooms.

In forgetting, a bear mother will storm some abandoned farm, astonished she made it without a rifle crack breaking her resolve. The compost pile will be full of fat grubs, crawling starbursts in her mouth. She will keep no superstitions, freed from the mermaids sutured on as a bargain. She will feed her cubs this simple paradise. Joy ache of slippers of fish slipping off healed limbs. New skin, tender but sturdy, like her young. She noses their bellies, wades in. Awake to the thin membrane of territory and perimeter and hillsides inlaid in ash that will be, one day,

erased.

Contributor's Note:
I grew up in Southern California and watched the news about the raging wildfires in late 2017 with a kind of frozen horror. The Thomas Fire that burned through Ventura and Santa Barbara counties and through Los Padres National Forest has since become California's largest wildfire on record, burning a staggering 281,893 acres during its stoic march through the hillsides. A story caught my eye in late January recounting efforts by wildlife officials to treat two black bears with terrible burns. They used a novel approach that involved putting sterilized tilapia fish skin on the burns. The collagen in the skin accelerates healing. Vets sewed on the fish skins and then wrapped the area with corn husks and rice skin. Two bears, one of them pregnant, underwent the procedure on their paws and have since been released.

The fish skin covered paws made me think of chimeras and something mythic and eternal, but it also had a temporary quality to it: the bandages would eventually wear out; the bear would be released and move on. This poem is an attempt to capture all those disparate elements.

Melinda Thomsen

In a Clearing by Taylor Creek

Fear bores into my soul
as you fire up a chain saw
to divide a pile of ten-foot-
long tree trunks.
I watch and will
the universe
to keep you safe.
Some logs have crumbled
from a legion of ants
that came before you
to make work easier.
The chain saw slips
through those ancient trunks
and I relax. You slice log
after log and the saw
buzzes on for hours.
Its noise lifts up
into the wide sky like a hand
trying to block out the sun
but the sun keeps shining
through spread fingers
and caresses the flush
of flowering weeds couched
at the far end of the enormous
timber pile. You move forward,
bole by bole, splitting cords
of firewood as the wind
tosses ironweed back
and forth, challenging
a honeybee but not
the monarch butterfly
who lands unaware
of gas fumes wafting
toward swaying wildflowers.

PHOTO BY JIM ROSS

PHOTO BY MARIA GREEN

Jennifer Falkner

Sometimes a Tree

—the trees are screaming. Many are still a haze of bare branches, even this late in May. If I had the equipment I would hear the air pockets form in the water column moving up their trunks, the inevitable result of prolonged drought. My work is farther up the mountain's slope, where pines and birches tend to crowd out the aspens.

There's a noise behind me, a gasping.

My neck prickles with sweat, even in the shade of the understory. A woman, pale as birch bark, leans against a balsam fir, dragging air into her lungs. It's one of those side effects of climate change no one saw coming. Everyone knew the milder winters were allowing parasites to thrive, and the absent songbirds meant more defoliation by caterpillars. With the drought in its third year, the trees are becoming increasingly maladapted to their environment. But of those remaining, no one expected quite so many of them to turn back into women.

"Shhh. You're breathing. You are. Just relax. You're here," I tell her.

It takes ages, but at last the woman's breathing begins to settle. Her heart no longer feels like a bird hurling itself against its cage, and I can stop rubbing circles on her back. She wipes tears away with her fists and straightens. She has the widest, greenest eyes I've ever seen. She's taller than me and her arms and legs are strangely elongated—they make me think of long grasses waving in the wind.

"Can I call someone? Take you somewhere?"

She speaks hesitantly, like a tourist trying on a new language. "No. I'm fine. Thank you."

"Here." I dig in my pack. "Some water. I'm Lois, by the way."

She takes the bottle reluctantly. Her hands are stiff, curled into themselves like the croziers of fiddleheads. It's impossible for her to unscrew the cap. A rush of warmth burns my cheeks, that feeling of looking after someone again. I open it for her. "What's your name?"

"Sylvie," she says. She's so thin. All I have is my pack of saplings, white pine from the southern states, and my own water ration. No food at all. And no clothes, other than the sweater I discarded this morning, oversized on me, but comically too short for her. She puts it on anyway.

I have to take her back down the trail to the bus. She stumbles a little over rocks in the path, so we take it slowly.

∞

When you were ten, Margo, you sized up every tree you came across. Was it sturdy enough to climb? Did it have a branch low enough to grasp, to begin the ascent?

There was a jack pine in the park behind the community centre where I brought you every Tuesday for gymnastics class. Pinus banksiana. *Its branches stuck out like the rungs of a ladder and its curling tip waved over the roof. The tallest tree in the park was always irresistible to you. All I could see was your favorite crimson T-shirt rising like a flag up a ship's mast. Occasionally an arm stuck out from the bristle-brush branches and waved. Other parents stopped, marveled, gave dire warnings. I could only breathe again when you were back on earth, sap smearing your shorts, a hitchhiking spider in your hair. How matter-of-factly you plucked it out.*

∞

When Sylvie and I reach the bus, I text Tom. The door is unlocked, so I can steal a spare T-shirt and shorts from one of the other planters, but without the keys, we'll have to wait until everyone returns before we can enjoy the air conditioning. There are six of us out here today, members of Regreen & Renew, volunteers connected with the government's program for assisted migration. But sitting with Sylvie in the bus's rectangle of shade, gazing at the sparkle of sunlight on the water through the pines, it feels like we're the only two people left in the world.

Tom's good with these girls. Mostly they fall in love with him. I'd fall in love with him, too, if I didn't remind myself every morning that I could be his mother. He takes them out, acclimatizes them to being with people again. I asked him once where he takes them; mostly they go for drinks at the Royal Oak. There's not much else to do around here.

A pileated woodpecker drills nearby, sharp-beaked and insistent.

"Does it hurt?" I touch her stiff fingers, half-expecting them to shrivel into themselves even more. Sylvie shrugs. "Is it arthritis?" Grandpa had arthritis but his claws looked nothing like this. "Maybe you should see a doctor . . ."

"No." She pulls away. "No doctors. I'm fine."

My turn to shrug. "Suit yourself."

Hands are unnecessary, she explains. They're a flourish, like the curlicues in fancy calligraphy. The real tools for survival are in her feet.

Only she calls them roots.

ান্তৰ-ণ্টৰ

I've had almost a year to put it together, Margo, the events of that night, from some of the people who were there and from everything you didn't say. Why didn't you tell me? In your tree-climbing days, you told me everything.

A party by the lake. End of term. You said it was just friends from school. I had no idea where it was, that it was so close to my grandparents' old sugar bush. You were almost home. But in the dark, in the unfaithful firelight that deepens the surrounding shadows, it was strange and new. Somebody brought a keg. Beer circulated in red plastic cups. Music drowned out the sounds of the night, the hooting owls, the coyotes. Maybe there were more people you didn't know than people you did. Students taking a break from tree planting. Newcomers from the drowning maritimes. But even people you knew became unrecognizable in the shifting orange light.

Then the snap of a twig from behind you. A body blocking your escape. Hands coming out of the dark, pushing you to the ground. How I wished you could scramble through the brush and find safety among the trees. But not everyone is so lucky.

At least Tom was there to bring you home.

ান্তৰ-ণ্টৰ

A text from Tom.

"He's on his way," I tell Sylvie. "You'll like him. He was one of my grad students. He's good at looking after people, even got me involved with Regreen & Renew."

This job was supposed to keep me from brooding. I thought there might have been some kind of redemption in my sunburned cheeks and nose, in my aching knees. Tom used to help me with my research, testing how quickly the mycorrhizal network sent messages from tree to tree, sending chemical warnings of approaching danger. I never thought of simply asking before.

"What was it like?"

"Pardon?"

"Being a tree. Did you and the other trees—communicate?"

She cocks her head. "I could feel them. They could feel me. We helped each other. It was like . . . buzzing? No, humming. We hummed together."

೮ঌ᠆ঌ৪

Before you left, it was becoming clear the Ottawa Valley was only going to get hotter and drier. I talked about moving. If we moved up north, where it used to be too cold to contemplate winter, we could just about keep the climate we were used to. Yes, there were blackflies and terrible roads and even more expensive groceries. But we could have our own sugar bush again. My grandparents' bush was already dying, barely producing enough sap for family use. I had stopped tapping completely. The trees needed it more.

You rolled your eyes. I had a lot of plans for us, and they usually involved some kind of running away, lighting out on our own, just us two. But you didn't want to leave then; you had a life here, and friends.

೮ঌ᠆ঌ৪

Tom comes huffing down the path towards us. He's wearing the same white Montreal Jazz Festival T-shirt he used to wear as an undergrad, worn gossamer-thin now and barely providing any protection against the sun.

"The others will be here soon," he says and smiles at Sylvie. He notices what I didn't, an ant struggling up her long hair, and pinches it away.

"Sylvie's staying with me tonight," I say. "I've got a pullout."

She looks at me. "A pullout?"

"My couch folds out into a bed."

Tom, the only one with a license to drive a bus, sticks the key in the ignition and turns up the air conditioning. We climb in after him.

೮ঌ᠆ঌ৪

You can tell most easily with quivering aspens. Populus tremuloides. Entire stands of them can be genetically identical, connected by a communicating root system. They're practically one organism, and, if undisturbed, they can live for hundreds, maybe thousands, of years. But in cases where the grove dies, from drought or disease, one or two trees may remain. Not flourishing, but dutifully pushing out the bare minimum of leaves each spring. There are support groups now, gathering around these outliers, but it's not an exact science.

Sometimes a tree is just a tree.

CR↬↭RD

Sylvie fits into your clothes so easily that for a second my eyes blur, for a second you are home again. But this never was your home, this one-bedroom apartment with the parking lot view. Your clothes, the ones you left behind, smell of the cardboard box I packed them in. The spare sheets smell like cardboard too. She crouches in front of the bookcase. All of your old books are there: paperback thrillers mostly; a couple biographies of your favourite singers, Lou Reed and David Bowie; travel guides from that year you spent traveling after high school. She pulls out *A Rough Guide for Thailand* and runs her fingers over its bright cover.

"Lois?"

I am staring.

"Mmm. Fine. Tom's coming by later. He wants to take you out for a drink."

There's hardly any natural light in the apartment, and by mid-afternoon it's already growing dim. I click on the light so she can read better.

I was always doing that.

CR↬↭RD

You were always going to leave. That was the deal, the one every parent knows from the beginning. But I was not prepared for the silence you left behind.

Tom and I had been testing the network, measuring how quickly and how far one tree could send out reserves of carbon and nitrogen to aid another in distress. In this case it meant injuring the trees ourselves, lopping off branches of some of the specimens of maple we planted last year. A long and difficult day. Tom was hungover. I had to snap at him for his sloppy note-taking, and then awkwardly apologize later, as we drove back to the city. I remember stopping on the way home for take-out to surprise you. Egg rolls and crispy beef, moo goo gai pan *and lemon chicken. All our old favourites, to tempt you out of your new reticence.*

You were already gone. Your guitar and most of your clothes. How matter-of-factly you plucked yourself out of my life.

CB ❧ ⚜ BO

The meteor shower is my idea. Sylvie never has much energy, but now she's growing listless. She stands in front of the sliding glass door to the balcony, practically motionless, for hours. It's not just the heat. It's not the process of adjustment. It's the acres of asphalt and cement in the city. It must be, because I feel it, too. There's a sick-looking Douglas fir that blocks almost all natural light from the living room, struggling on in its small patch of lawn. I think she's keeping it company. We need to get out of here.

Tom hasn't been around in a few days, and I wonder if he and Sylvie had an argument. They're both so careful not to mention each other's name.

His voice is wary when I call, but when I suggest the trip, he pounces on the opportunity. Thank goodness, because we need to drive miles from the city to get away from the light pollution and the heat. I don't have a car.

CB ❧ ⚜ BO

I used to wish you and Tom would get together. He's only a couple of years older. He's bright. And he'd keep you close to me. You wanted nothing to do with him. You said there was something sleazy in the way he looked after the girls from the woods. And then, after the party, you refused to mention him at all. It was easy to pretend not to notice.

It was safer.

CB ❧ ⚜ BO

There are a couple of other cars here, in the small gravel parking lot designated a Dark Sky Zone. Sylvie draws away from Tom's car, to the tall grasses and scrub, to the edge of the wilderness. If possible, she looks even thinner than when I found her. The moonless night is loud with cicadas and the high whine of mosquitoes. Almost immediately my skin feels like it is crawling with insects.

"Hang on, I've got some bug spray." Tom limps round to the trunk and rummages around inside.

"Tom, what's wrong with your foot?"

"Nothing."

I can barely make out the other people here. Some are standing by their cars, others have moved out to the edge of the lot. They are like shadows, as still and silent as Sylvie, all of them gazing in expectation to the northeast. The air is thick and humid and tinged with the smell of wet wood, of something rotten.

I lower my voice. "No, really. What happened?"

"Splinters. Should've put some shoes on, I guess. Found it!" He brandishes the plastic bottle.

"Splinters?" I ask too loudly. There is a shushing from the shadows.

"Don't laugh," he whispers.

He was able to remove three of them, he says, but the rest are too deeply embedded. But wood is organic and so is he. They'll dissolve eventually.

"But . . . what were you doing to get the splinters in the first place?"

He glances at Sylvie, whose back is towards us.

I try to make out his expression, to work out what he's not telling me. But now that the interior light from the car has turned off, there is only the Milky Way above us and intermittent blinking of fireflies, out earlier than ever this year. Tom is invisible. All I see is a tall, blocky figure moving towards Sylvie. A hand reaching out of the dark.

I can't look away anymore. I can't pretend not to see.

I remind myself that we are surrounded by people. Even if they seem as self-contained as a forest, they are still here. I am not alone. I step forward, blocking his way.

"You should go."

"What?"

"Go home, Tom. You need to leave us alone." I am not whispering anymore.

"Lois, you can't be serious."

I pull out my phone. "I'll call the police if I have to."

People are turning, watching us. Sylvie's hand slips into mine. Her stiff fingers wriggle and uncurl, just a little. Air pockets move just below the surface of her skin. She is still screaming, but now, I can hear her.

"We'll find our own way home. Without you."

CB ふ～らⓈBひ

The stars are so close, their suspension in the black sky such a tenuous thing. One swift breeze and they'll scatter like snow. I miss you so much it's hard to breathe.

This time I promise, Margo, I promise I won't let go—

Laurie Kolp

Released from the Bondage of Self

Bare-kneed kneeling in gravel, god-gazing the slow cloud,
my life is not my life. I have no life apart from
the four dimensions of breathing,
face melting down to the last puff
of peppered breeze—
easier to float above
the plinth of greater things than me.

Cento Credits:

L1- Lauren Gordon, Missing Woman Unwittingly Joins Search Party Looking for Herself

L2- Li-Young Lee, Spoken For

L3- Ilya Kaminsky, A Toast

L4- Charles Bukowski, Something for the Touts, the Nuns, the Grocery Clerks, and You . . .

L5- Patricia Smith, Incendiary Art

L6- Avery M. Guess, The Body Keeps the Score

L7- Li-Young Lee, Spoken For

Travis Truax

Wicker

The dead will always shame the living.
I can't begin to count the ways, so please

don't ask. Tonight a dozen ravens jump ship

from a sea of cirrus and snowy streetlamps.
Not a one balks at the passing cars or sings.

I watch the bluest grey slowly bed-down to sleep.

When the season becomes nothing but new gloves,
I leave the car in the garage and wait for spring.

When the inky ash branches crawl too high,
I stoop along the sidewalk and remember school.

Once, I took pride in knowing every state.
I rode the breakwaters of the multiplication table.

Now I count the minutes before work and scribble
what I can from this mess. Steady patterns

pulled from the wicker house of luck and loss,
no matter the cataclysms that connect it.

Someone once told me they could live in Iowa,
if it weren't for winter and all the twisters.

I couldn't agree less. Nothing lives the life
we imagine. Not even ravens. Not even yesterday.

PHOTO BY TRAVIS VOLK

Theodora Goss

In the Forest of Forgetting

Originally printed in Realms of Fantasy. *Reprinted with author's permission.*

She stood at the edge of the forest. She knew it was the edge because behind her the path disappeared into undergrowth. She could see rhododendrons, covered with flowers like cotton candy. There were bushes without flowers, which she could not name: *shrubus leafiana*. Ahead of her, the path was shadowed by oaks, poplars, maples with leaves like Canadian flags. In the shadow of the trees, the air was cool and smelled of toothpaste.

"Welcome," said the Witch. She was standing beneath an oak tree whose branches were covered with green acorns. The Witch was wearing a white coat. Around her neck was a silver chain, with a silver disk hanging from it. Just what a Witch should look like, she thought. It was comforting when things looked as they should. The forest, for instance.

"Where am I?" she asked.

"In the Forest of Forgetting," said the Witch. "Hence the forgetting. Let me check your heart."

"Why am I here?"

The Witch placed the silver disk on her chest. It felt cold against her bare skin. "Heart normal. You're here because you have lumps."

She looked down at her chest, where the silver disk had been placed. There they were, the only lumps she could see, above the slight bulge of her stomach.

"What's wrong with them?" They were small and a bit crooked, but they looked all right.

The Witch put her hands in her pockets. "Your lumps have metastasized. They must be removed."

"Well," she said. And again, "Well." Even in the stillness under the trees, which made her feel calm and a bit sleepy, this seemed unnecessarily repetitive. "How—"

"With this," said the Witch, pulling a silver wand from one pocket. It looked harmless enough. The Witch muttered something under her breath and waved her wand.

Before she had time to close her eyes or prepare herself for whatever might happen, two moths rose from her chest, white with flecks of gray on their wings. They fluttered along the path, looping and twisting around one another, as though making invisible macrame.

She looked down at her chest. The lumps were gone.

"That went quite well," said the Witch, replacing the wand in her pocket.

The moths fluttered upward, spiraling into the treetops until she could no longer see them. The clouds overhead were white and fluffy, like sheep. No, she thought. Like pillows, like unrolled toilet paper left in heaps on the floor. She liked creating unusual similes.

"Don't go too far into the forest," said the Witch. "You'll have to come back, eventually." The Witch began walking toward the rhododendrons and nameless bushes.

"Wait," she said. Something had been bothering her. She had almost forgotten it, watching the moths rise upward. "What is my name?"

The Witch turned back for a moment. Her silver disk winked in the shifting light under the trees. "Your name is Patient."

She looked down at the path: her feet were bare, and her toenails needed clipping. That didn't sound right at all. She wasn't particularly patient, was, in fact, generally impatient. She looked up, wanting to ask the Witch if she were certain, but the Witch was gone.

There was nothing to do but go farther into the forest. It was silent, except for the occasional rustle high among the treetops.

☙❧

When she heard laughter, she looked up. In the branches of a laurel, spiders had woven their webs, like a giant game of cat's cradle. They were brown, and about the size of her hand.

"What sort of web? What web? What web?" The words came down

to her in clacking sing-song, as though she were being questioned by a collection of sewing machines. One spider spun itself down from a branch and hung by its thread in front of her. "What web?" It went into paroxysms of laughter, shaking on its thread like a brown yo-yo.

She looked around her, trying to see what the spiders were laughing about, and saw that the path behind her was littered with brown string. She knelt down, picked up a handful, and suddenly realized what she was holding

"Not a web," she said to the spiders. "My hair. See?" She put her hand on her head. It was bare. Her arms and legs were bare. Even the place under her belly was bare. "It's fallen out. I won't have to buy shampoo or disposable razors." She said this to show it was probably for the best. Perhaps they believed her, because their laughter stopped and the dangling spider rose again to his branch. But she sat on the path and cried, wiping her eyes with a handful of hair.

When she was finished, she blew her nose on an oak leaf and went on. It was no use, she told herself, crying over spilt hair. Perhaps she would grow a winter coat. Perhaps it would come in white, like an arctic hare's.

CB ~⌥€

She was so focused on planning for winter, when her coat would come in and she would live on acorns, that she almost tripped over the coffin.

"Be careful," said the first Apprentice. He was dressed in a blue coat, and wore a blue shower cap on his head. Around his neck was a silver chain, with a silver disk hanging from it.

"You'll trip over the Queen," said the second Apprentice, who was dressed just like him.

"If you tripped, she would blame us," said the third Apprentice. Her shower cap was pushed back to show her bangs.

"Who?" she asked. "The Queen?" The Queen looked incapable of blaming anybody.

"The Witch. We're her Apprentices," said the Apprentices together.

"Obviously," muttered the third Apprentice.

She wondered if they had practiced beforehand.

"Let us check your heart," said the first Apprentice. All three came together and put their silver disks on her chest.

"Heart normal."

"Too slow."

"Too fast."

They glared at each other and began arguing among themselves.

She looked down at the Queen. The glass of the coffin was perfectly clear. Through it she could see the Queen's robe, a deep blue, and her blue turban. Her face was a little blue as well.

"She died of lumps," said the Apprentices.

"They metastasized."

"The Witch could not remove them in time."

"Magic is much more advanced, nowadays."

She put her hands on the coffin and, not knowing what else to do, tapped her fingers on the glass. Her cuticles were ragged. What would the Queen think?

"She left you gifts," said the Apprentices.

"A dress." It was made of paper, and tied in back. She could not reach the strings, so the first Apprentice tied it for her. She had never liked floral patterns, she thought, looking down at herself. But it would have to do until her winter coat came in.

"A mirror." The second Apprentice held it for her. She realized, with surprise, that she had no eyebrows. She should have expected that. It made her look surprised, which seemed appropriate.

The third Apprentice smiled and said, "You look a little like her, only not so blue."

She did, indeed, look a little like the Queen. "Thank you," she said. The Queen approved of politeness. "Did she, by any chance, leave me a name?" She did not want to seem ungrateful, but this was, after all, important to her. You needed a name, if someone was going to, for example, ask you to lunch. She had not eaten since breakfast, and she was beginning to feel hungry.

"Your name is Daughter," they said. "Now it's time to turn back."

"Why?" Surely she was too old for a name like Daughter.

They looked at each other, then muttered among themselves. "Because," they said decisively.

She frowned, wondering what it looked like without eyebrows, wondering if she should look in the mirror again to find out. Instead, she turned and walked farther along the path, deeper into the forest.

"Wait!" they shouted behind her.

"You're going too far!"

"Your heart can't take it!"

"Do you want to end up like the Queen?"

Eventually, it was silent again.

❦

The forest began to grow darker. Maples and poplars were replaced by pines. Needles prickled her feet as she walked on the path. She tried to eat a pinecone, but it left her hands sticky and tasted like gasoline. Not that she had tasted gasoline, but she imagined it would taste exactly like that. If she could wash her hands in the river—

"No one may cross the river," said the Knight.

"I don't want to cross. I just want to wash my hands and have a drink."

"No," said the Knight. Above the knees, he was dressed in a suit of armor. Below, he wore a pair of galoshes. "Ouyay aymay otnay inkdray oray ashway. Onay Oneway." He lifted his visor. His mustache looked like it had been cut with nail clippers. It was turning gray.

"Why?" It was the question she had been asking since she entered the forest.

The Knight looked puzzled. "I don't know. I think it's a rule or something." He had a nice voice. The Witch and her Apprentices had sounded like subway conductors. And the Queen hadn't spoken at all. "I think you're supposed to go back."

"That's just it," she said. "Who is you? I mean, who is me?" She sounded impatient, and she realized that she must be: hungry, tired, impatient. No one in this forest answered questions directly. Would anyone tell her what she wanted to know?

"Well," he said. He tugged at his mustache, although his armored hands were clumsy. "You like blackberry pie. You overwater houseplants, feed stray cats on the back porch, sleep through your alarm clock." He began counting on his fingers. It must help him remember, she thought. "You write stories for children: *A Camembert Moon*, *Priscilla's Flying Pig*, *The Train to Nowhereton*. You complain about your knees, and you hate wearing glasses. Once, you went on a diet where you ate nothing but cucumbers for a week. You can't mend socks, play tennis, or sing. You hate scrubbing toilets." He reached ten and looked at her, fingers outspread. "How am I doing?"

"Well," she said. She did like blackberry pie, although she didn't need glasses. Her eyesight was perfectly clear. She could see, for instance, that the Knight had wrinkles under his eyes. They made him look rather handsome. "But what is my name?"

"I think," said the Knight, looking at his fingers as though trying to remember. "I think your name is Wife."

It was a nice name, whispery, like "wish" and "whinny" and "willow." It was the nicest name she had heard so far. But it wasn't quite right.

"I'm sorry," she said, because the Knight was looking at her with an anxious smile. She stepped into the river.

"Wait!" said the Knight.

The river was cold and clear and shallow. Although there were stepping stones, she walked on the muddy bottom, letting the water curl around her ankles, then around her knees. In the middle of the river, she bent down to wash her hands and frightened a brown fish under a rock. Once her hands were no longer sticky, she drank from them and splashed water on her face, scattering drops of water on her paper dress.

"Won't you reconsider?" shouted the Knight. He was standing in the water, up to the buckles of his galoshes. She wondered if he would follow her into the river, but he did not. Perhaps, she thought, he was afraid that his armor would rust. Instead, he stood near the riverbank, arms held out like an airplane. He was standing there each time she turned back to look. Finally, the path bent and she could no longer see him.

⚜

Once, a family of squirrels scrambled down from an oak tree and asked for her autograph. The squirrel children had copies of *A Camembert Moon*. When she told them she had no pen, they brought her berries. She signed each one "With regards, Author." She wondered where they kept books, whether there were shelves in the oak tree. When she had signed copies for Jumpy, Squirmy, Tailless, Nuthunter, and Squawk, they shared their dinner with her: an acorn mash that would have made a good meal, if she had been a squirrel. She was still hungry, although less hungry than before.

⚜

Finally, the trees grew farther apart. She saw undergrowth, including a bush with berries. They looked like the berries the squirrels had used for ink. She wondered if they were safe to eat, and thought of trying a few. Surely if they were poisonous she would feel sick or throw up. A few would not kill her. But she was too nervous to try.

The trees ended at the edge of a meadow filled with Queen Anne's lace, poppies, cornflowers. And beyond the meadow—

"Are you going to the mountains?" asked the Princess. She wore pajamas with feet and a necklace of paperclips.

Was she? They were blue with pines, and probably farther away than they appeared.

"Look at what I have," said the Princess. She was holding a wicker cage. In it were two moths, white with gray markings on their wings.

"I wondered where they had gone," she said. She was sorry, now, to have lost them. They were pretty, like sheets of newspaper turned into kites.

"I'll give them water in the teacups my dolls use. Do you know my dolls?"

"No," she said. It was an important question: was she going to the mountains?

"Their names are Octavia, because she only has eight toes, and Puddle. Because you know." The Princess raised her hand to her mouth, as though speaking through a trumpet. "She's just a baby."

"Do you like making dresses for your dolls?" she asked the Princess.

"Yes," said the Princess. "I make them from leaves and toilet paper."

"If you help me untie it," she said, "you can have my dress." It had been itching for some time, and anyway she would not need it in the mountains. When the strings were untied, she slipped the dress off and handed it to the Princess.

Someone was moving in the meadow, someone in a blue coat, with a blue shower cap on his head. He was holding an enormous butterfly net. And another someone, and another.

"We'll catch her!" shouted the Apprentices, jumping and turning as though chasing enormous butterflies.

"She shouldn't have crossed the river!"

"Her heart can't take the strain!"

"But we'll catch her here, never worry!"

Had she made her final decision? Was she going to the mountains? The Apprentices began stalking away from each other, like detectives.

"You're good at names, aren't you?" she said to the Princess.

The Princess nodded. "I once named seventeen caterpillars. They were named one, two, three, four, five, and so on, up to seventeen."

"What would you name me?" Every few minutes, one Apprentice would run up to another, shouting "Boo!" and making the other jump. The mountains looked mysterious and inviting.

The Princess considered. "I think I would name you Mother."

"An excellent name." But not her name, not quite. She would find her name in the mountains. It would be unexpected and inevitable, a name she could never have imagined, like Rumpelstiltskin. In the mountains she would learn about berries. Her winter coat would come in.

She leaned down and kissed the Princess, then put one hand on the wicker cage. "Goodbye," she said. "Take good care of them. I think they once belonged to the Queen."

She stepped into the sunlight. It was warm on her body. Bees circled around her, visiting the Queen Anne's lace. The Apprentices were stalking away from each other, butterfly nets raised and fluttering in the breeze. She hoped they would not notice her.

She held out her hands so they brushed the tops of the grasses, and started across the meadow.

Abigail Warren

The Table-Setter

Feelings were the fork
set to the left of the plate
sadness was a knife

on the right;
She spooned out joy,
in small mouthfuls,

cut a slice of pride,
when you came to the table.
Labeled it in the photograph album

afterward.
It made everything clear
for everyone in her family.

Like reading the label
on the prescription bottle:
may cause vomiting,

or feelings of euphoria.
It went on like this
for years

that clarity of emotion;
Until truth spilled
across the table

running in the napkins
dripping on laps, then
all over the floor.

She was angry

angry with death
staining the tablecloth.

They wrapped her
in it, said good-bye.
Went back to the empty

table. Feasted on air.

PHOTO BY RUSSELL WILSON

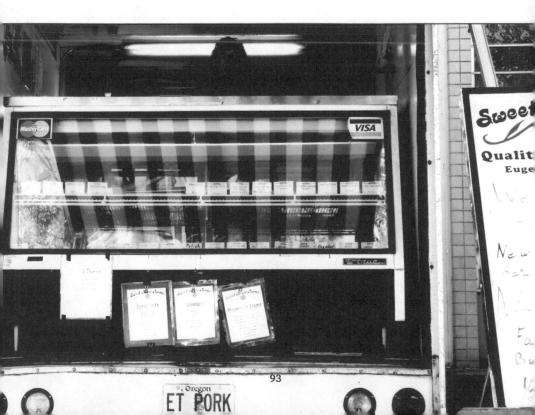

PHOTO BY MARIA GREEN

Madeline Miele

An Argument Against Morning Eggs

You make my eggs sunny
side up without asking how
I want them. I know I've made
it clear how I feel about eating
babies for breakfast. Crack of
the shell, shell in the bin, butter
in the pan, egg in the pan, yellow
yolk on a wide dinner plate.
Ice pops from a stream in the
woods in the hollow white of
winter. Water runs under ice. Snow
grows heavy on a branch in the
woods and falls. Water rushes
through the hole made in the ice
by the branch in the woods without
an audience. We see velvet blackness
where we don't know ice used to be.
I want cereal to punctuate the silence
but I don't say so. You're pouring
grease from the pan into a jelly jar.
It's getting warm again. Newborn
leaves press against the kitchen
window. It's selfish the way that yolk
steals all the light from the room.

Carina Bissett

Cracked

Helen stayed stoic throughout her labor, but when the doctor finally settled a large egg on her stomach instead of the red-faced, squalling infant she'd been expecting, her composure finally broke. It began with tears and escalated into hysterical laughter. The attending nurse, an old battle-axe, gave her a reproachful look and muttered something about first-time, middle-aged mothers before whisking the egg to safety. After a few minutes Helen's laughter shifted back to sobs, which eventually wound down to a desultory silence.

She had prepared for a natural delivery. After Dan left, she instead opted for an epidural. The anesthesiologist told her she was fine, but Helen insisted she was having some sort of weird reaction to the pain medications. She sulked in her bed as the nurses cooed over the "little darling" in the bassinet. No one told her how brave she was. No one marveled over her impossible delivery of a ten-pound *egg*. In fact, no one gave her any attention at all.

At the nurses' insistence, Helen forced herself to hold the swaddled bundle, but she immediately deposited it back into the bassinet as soon as they left. Each time she handled the egg, she remembered the damn "egg baby" assignment she'd failed in junior high home economics. Back then, she only had to care for a hollowed-out chicken egg. But after she crushed the second one in less than an hour, the teacher gave her a "flour baby" to take care of instead. At the end of the unit, she turned in a plate of chewy brownies wrapped in an empty flour sack. The teacher wasn't amused. Helen took that lesson to heart: babies will ruin your life, not to mention your GPA.

A nurse half her age came into the room with discharge papers. The woman was dressed in seasonally pastel scrubs decorated with pink bunnies and colored eggs, her identification badge covered with snapshots of bright-eyed toddlers. Helen glanced from those pictures to the massive egg propped up in the beige car carrier. Maybe Dan hadn't been the father after all. Maybe some kinky Greek god had visited her in the guise of a bird. Not that she'd willingly fuck a bird. Would she? Thinking about it made Helen's head hurt.

"It's hard work, especially for a woman your age." The young nurse winked knowingly as she snapped pink gum between even white teeth. "Do you have a name picked out?"

Helen bristled. Of course she had names picked out. She was a logical woman who worked with numbers and charts on a daily basis. But there was nothing normal about her current situation. The names she'd selected all had specific meanings. She had one for a girl and one for a boy and even had a second of each just in case twins showed up. Surprises happen, right? But none of those carefully collated monikers would work for an egg. What were the alternatives? Shelby? Egbert? Benedict? The whole situation was ridiculous.

She finally settled on Pascal, a nod to her favorite philosopher-mathematician, but left the box denoting the father blank. When she got home Helen took Pascal straight to the nursery she'd so painstakingly decorated in neutral shades of cream and tan. The understated, yet elegant toile wallpaper featured characters from the classic Mother Goose nursery rhymes—"Humpty Dumpty" was, of course, included.

Helen sighed and lowered Pascal into the crib. The smooth shell gleamed.

She decided to change the nursery's theme to something bold and bright, dinosaurs perhaps. With that, she kissed Pascal good night and turned out the lights.

Over the next few days Helen rigorously researched everything she could find on how to hatch eggs. She discovered that the largest eggs on land came from ostriches, but Pascal's size broke all records. The horrifying discovery led to a whiskey-fueled inspection of her lady bits with a hand mirror. Whether it was the booze or the low lighting, the damage wasn't as extensive as she'd feared. Even so, Helen decided Pascal would just have to deal with being an only child.

Stable in the career she'd built over two decades, Helen decided to continue her work as a tax accountant from home. The regular pedicures, injections, and salon visits resumed; however, this time she had the stylists come to her. And, although she never experienced a rush of maternal love, Helen excelled at caring for Pascal's physical needs as she excelled at each endeavor she undertook.

In her off-hours Helen began to redecorate the nursery. Unwilling to deal with the mess and hassle of live plants, she draped green silk tacked to the ceiling. For a bit of added flair, she pinned on dozens of fabric leaves—quilted maple, beaded aspen, embroidered palm. The baby swing and changing table she replaced with large stuffed dinosaurs custom ordered to match the blue-green leaves and orange blooms in the jungle-themed curtains. The crib she dismantled as well. In its place, she pieced together designer pillows and sheets to form a nest large enough for her to rest comfortably. Whenever she began to feel broody, she'd climb in and curl up with Pascal, basking in the warmth of the grow lights hanging in every corner.

The egg still hadn't hatched after forty-five days. That's when Helen decided they both needed some fresh air. She used organic makeup to create a face for Pascal. The eyes were lopsided, but adorable in their own way. She tucked the swaddled egg into the new stroller she'd modified with a portable heating blanket. After a quick touch-up with a lipstick pencil and a swipe of gloss, Pascal was deemed presentable and off they went.

Two houses away, a woman blocked their path on the sidewalk. She was dressed in stained clothing and cradled a bulging sling tied across her chest.

"Makeup on a baby?" the stranger gasped. "What kind of monster are you?"

The question startled Helen, who'd been minding her own business, thinking about the potential of natural dyes to give Pascal a more sophisticated look.

Helen wrinkled her nose at the disheveled and obviously distraught young woman. Even from the distance of a few feet, there was a strong smell like talcum powder, sour milk, and urine. Totally unprovoked, a baby began to cry, a loud whooping wail. The sling distorted as the creature inside struggled for immediate attention. Horrified, Helen took advantage of the distraction and continued on her way, prim heels clicking against the sidewalk. As she rounded the corner, she shook her head in disgust.

Some women just weren't meant to be mothers.

Helen Waters

Emus

My stepuncle Randy was one of those people who thought that emu farming was the next big thing in American agriculture. He lost a bunch of his family's money on his failed emu farm venture, including some of my stepdad's.

A few times at dinner, there would be a funny taste to my spaghetti with meat sauce, and I'd ask my mother accusingly if I was eating emu. It was always a sore subject. My mom wanted to use the emu meat to make my stepdad feel better about his brother's failure. I didn't want to eat emu.

There was a lot of it, ground and vacuum-packed, in the deep freeze in the utility room.

Free association:

    Uncle Randy - rat tail
    Uncle Randy - trailer home
    Uncle Randy -
    Uncle Randy - Betty
    Uncle Randy - pyramid scheme

We went to visit the farm once. It was kind of like Jurassic Park, if Jurassic Park had only blue-green ostrich dinosaurs. Tall fences. Mean creatures.

At the end there was one emu left over, and he came to live with us. He lived in our front pasture, sharing it with the horses. Then he cut his neck on the barbed wire fence and when he ate, the food pellets would fall out of the cut in his neck, so he died.

PHOTO BY TRAVIS VOLK

PHOTO BY MARIA GREEN

Sarah Broussard Weaver

Green House, on Bayou Lafourche

Dark cool kitchen, Mawmaw the resident queen
unless Pawpaw was making his healthy
brown bread that I hated.
Good for the body, give you muscles, he said.

See: the dish drainer held a condensing two-liter plastic bottle,
recycled before the bayou had bins. Its crystal chunk of ice
slowly melted, releasing cold sweet water to drip into autumnal
Tupperware cups, avocado green, burnt orange, mustard yellow—
shades of the seventies. My sister and I still had dry tongues.

On the same counter, a plastic ice cream bucket now held scraps
collected from dinner plates for the chicken pen out back.
One day I loitered, smelling sweet-peas, and saw the delivery,
Pawpaw with the bucket, scraping out roasted chicken and rice.
I told mom it was wrong and gross, making cannibals of choiceless chickens.

Imagine it: the chickens ate their friends and family, who became a part of them,
later were consumed themselves, people getting first gnawings, chickens second.
Eventually, when I ate Pawpaw's roasted chicken, I could be eating the lives of ten
chickens or more. A strange circle of power reclaimed and reused.

At the end of the day the two-liter received new water,
poured on top of the star-shot chunk remaining.
Frozen overnight in the old brown refrigerator—those autumn colors again—with
a felt barnyard magnet: *Holy Cow! Are you eating again?*
Miss Cow was depicted eating a pink flower—a lovely feminine thing to consume.
She could righteously speak to the situation.

Alyssa Hamilton

The Barn Beyond

Mama and Papa keep wiping tears away. I don't know why they gotta do that. Nana is just gonna be stuffed full of straw, and she'll keep the crows from spookin' the cows. I told them that, but Mama just started crying all over again, breathed real fast like inout inout. Papa said to go outside. Gotothebarn. Talk to your pigeon friends.

It's cold.

The cows scatter their beds, sticking out the snow. I give big armfuls of barley to keep 'em warm, but some of them eat it instead. All of them are named bessie. Bessie bessie bessie, mooing and curdling in s l o w m o t i o n. Got brains made of cheese. Nana, is God gonna give you a brand new brain [all WizardofOz] [or all zombie if she eats it like dust]? But you already had brains, that's what the movie says. Had brains the whole time. Nana, when you gonna be that scarecrow?

When they gonna stick you in the ground? Where they gonna do it?

Papa tried to say that Nana is going to Heaven. Heaven is white like snow and milk and fur washed and clean dishes. Is the straw gonna be white? Or still yellow? Jesus has a yellow halo at church. Papa's been there a lot. He takes me with him since Mama don't like to go. I sit next to him as he mumbles at the candles. The candles are white. The light is yellow. Maybe Nana will be white and yellow since that's Heaven. The air smells stale like the Communion wafers. It smells funny like you used to.

I climb up to the loft. Hay pokes at me when I sit. Nana, is that you? You already being made into a scarecrow? Nana, does it hurt you, being

made of straw? Hurt less than the c-a-n-c-e-r? More? Is the straw soft in Heaven? Papa says Heaven is being happy with all the angels. Are the angels sewing you together now?

I look out the window. The clouds roll over the sun. The cows are stayin' close together. Their tails flick. Some are lying down. Black and white circles, all around the new scarecrow. It looks like a coat propped up in the middle. Got a big red hat. Even got a hump like Nana had.

Nana, did you know you were gonna die when Papa and I started to make the scarecrow? You said the crows were hoppin' too close. That why you wanted to see pictures of it? So you'd see how you'd look after the c—a—n—c—e—r? Would it scare that away, too?

A crow lands on new Nana. The cows go moomoomoo. Oh bessie bessie bessie calm down; it's just a silly bird [justasillybird]. It ain't gonna hurt you. Nana, you ain't supposed to make friends with the crows. You gotta be mean to 'em. I know you don't wanna be. Prolly wanna give 'em hard candies and tell 'em to keep quiet about it to your mom. Can you still wink with a button-eye?

"Nana!" I call out. Another crow lands on her hat. "Scare it! Scare it away!"

Nothin.

I don't think she can hear me anymore.

PHOTO BY JEFFREY ALFIER

Candelin Wahl

Unexpected

Humdrum green carpeting muffled
the bathroom tucked under the eaves
of our second floor flat. A maid's room

in a former time, its low window granted
a Lake Champlain view once you were seated.
New maternity tops hung in the roomy closet.

Like a Martha Stewart protégé,
I crafted a rolling shade in there—
the fabric sea of violets gave me joy.

Twelve weeks sprouted, your father
trumpeted you—to the mailman, the boss,
the butcher at Longe Brothers Market.

> the midwife said stay home
> rest—maybe the bleeding will stop
> when the waves started
> I curled on the mossy rug
> like a yearling doe in the forest
> my cheek pressed against the cool
> tub, praying to freeze frame your
> sonogram self

We read all the books, dreamed
you floating into a warm bath
like a Hawaiian newborn.

You had a different story to write.
I birthed what little there was
of you into the porcelain bowl.

Devin Donovan

On the Eve of All Saints' Eve

My wife and I are having a party tonight. Call it a date night. The four dogs will be there. We will snuggle. On the couch, in the basement, we will eat ice cream.

Maybe we will watch some episodes of *The Office*.

It is October 30—tomorrow will be Halloween, then All Saints Day, and then All Souls Day after that. It's a spectral stretch of calendar.

∞≈∞

When I was just a kid, my mother threw a combined birthday party for my two dead sisters. Karol was born lifeless in 1978 with the umbilical cord wrapped around her neck like a noose; two years later Margaret Mary passed away when she was only four days old. They became guardian angels. They hovered over me and my brother like cherubs, older than babies, but still radiating a newborn innocence.

These girls were so sweet that on the day when we celebrated our memory of them—maybe only our knowledge of their names, really— they gave both me and my brother presents. The gifts were bestowed, like a protective gaze, upon us as younger siblings, even though we were older now than they would ever be. One year—let's say I was seven years old—my mother gave me a large, flat, wooden wreath painted baby blue. It was addressed to me from Karol and Margaret Mary. In the center of the hollow circle, a small wood cutout of a pair of baby booties swung by a short length of rope. Around the wreath in white lettering, encircling the swinging booties, it read:

God Danced the Day You Were Born.

My little brother—he would have been four—got a pair of *official* Ninja Turtle pajamas. Michelangelo's signature orange belt ran across the muscular turtle belly with screen-print nunchakus tucked at the hip. He put them on as soon as they were out of the box, and I watched him leap around the room while my wreath lay flat and useless on the table.

Looking from the pajamas to my wreath, in that moment, I knew the great indifference of the universe. I threw what can only be described as a biblical tantrum; there was wailing and gnashing of teeth. I sobbed and snarled about how the wreath didn't do anything but sit there. You couldn't even play with it.

I didn't care if God danced—*he wasn't a Ninja Turtle.*

To this day, I cannot imagine the sadness this must have caused my mother. She tried to commemorate two lost daughters by making them a part of two sons' happiness. I said *not good enough.* I wonder if my mother thought about a trade in that moment, if she tried to imagine what Karol or Margaret Mary would have done in my place. Would they have been as ungrateful as I was, had I died and given them a gift? I wonder if she looked at me and thought about how she didn't get to choose who her children were. Or, if she didn't think these thoughts, I wonder what she did to hold them back.

C3 ∂∽⟨S 80

My mother always told me that I was sent by God to take her tears away, and I would say "with a brush." And she would laugh a sweet laugh, and, even if her eyes watered a bit, it was like I could see the brush in my hand every time.

Because I made my mother so happy after my two baby sisters had made her so sad, I have always suspected that I was somehow responsible for their deaths. Like my soul, or the idea of my future existence, had killed them off to make room for me—had created a void in my mother's heart into which I swooped, like some kind of savior. Other times I felt like I swallowed my sisters, absorbed them—made their baby souls, their potential, their quirks and their futures a part of my own being, my own story.

Either way, I know I owe two lives.

My name sits heavy in the right column of some cosmic ledger. No one has yet come to collect. When they do, what would I even pay?

CB&~&80

Last month, my younger brother—now grown out of those Ninja Turtle pajamas—texted a picture of his fiancée's twelve-week sonogram to the eleven people on our family text chain. It buzzed my wife's phone while she was at the doctor's appointment where a vaginal ultrasound showed abnormalities at eight weeks.

It could be nothing, the OB told her, *or it could be the early signs of miscarriage.* Another miscarriage. Two in a row. *It's a wait and see.*

The sonogram looks like a total solar eclipse. It is a ring of light with a spot of brilliance, like an inset diamond. I point to the diamond and ask my wife if that's the abnormality. *It's the heartbeat,* she tells me, *we'll know more in two weeks.*

CB&~&80

Tonight is the night before Halloween, two weeks and three days after the sonogram. We are having a party. Only the dogs are invited.

We might watch *The Office.*

At the appointment three days ago, the OB explained that my wife could either have surgery to remove the unviable pregnancy or take pills to help it pass. It might cause infection if it remains inside her body. It does not pass like our first miscarriage, in the bathroom of my brother's apartment, at my sister's bridal shower.

My wife is instructed to lie down after inserting the pills; when they kick in, they will wrack her womb with contractions. Her whole body will tighten and relax like a pulsing fist, all to move a little diamond ring. We'll be on our bed. She'll squeeze my hand and I'll rub her back. But that's hours from now.

Right now, Tibbon and Caddy and Rosie and Petunia and I snuggle her body as it prepares for difficult work. I guess at her mind, and write down my own.

If God danced the day I was born, what did he do when Karol was born still? And on Margaret Mary's fourth and final day?

What are God's feet up to tonight?

Roselyn Kubek

Eating Grief

That winter my husband brews
chicken broth with schmaltz, garlic, marrow,
pleads,
Eat.

Neighbors leave casseroles,
swaddled infants on our front steps.
I arrange them; our table looks fed.

When he works again, I bake bread.
Yeast rises. I taste steam,
trash the loaf;
let him think I ate it.

Soon I'm hollow as balsa.

By March, they make me rest,
make sure I swallow enough
fistfuls of Cheerios.

That June, I stumble in untended gardens,
trip on fruit-burdened vines, fall
into brambles, raise angry
welts.

I want to stomp muddy pulp,
pluck and mash fat drupelets
between my fingers,
lick blue-black rivulets
that snake down my wrist,
suck the sour
sweet as venom
after months of salt.

When I finally disentangle,
I do it slowly, spit out
not one dark seed.

PHOTO BY MARIA GREEN

C.R. Beideman

Pinewood Derby

Make a little birdhouse in your soul.
They Might Be Giants

The morning smelled like grass clippings and sulfur. Toothpaste foamed in Blaise's mouth as his brush swished over molars. He lowered his chin and spat and sucked water from the faucet with the shiny blue racer rotating on display in his mind. In the basement below, his block of pinewood waited.

Blaise went to the kitchen and ate cornflakes. He crunched and crunched, muting his family's chatter. Sister and Mom appeared wide-eyed and trembling. Dad's jaw moved slowly, but his foot bobbed fast under the table. Blaise was sure blue was the right color—blue, with one silver racing stripe.

Behind Mom, the window shattered.

Glass caught in her thick hair and a black bible thudded on the linoleum floor. Sister led Mom toward the bathroom. Dad knocked the table as he rose, telling the boy to go with Mom. Blaise rinsed his bowl in the sink and walked toward the basement.

In the living room, he stopped to pet the cat. "Meow meow," Blaise said. Then he turned the basement door's faceted glass knob. The hinges creaked shut as he stepped down rough wooden stairs in stale darkness until a string danced on his face. He tugged twice and a yellow bulb hummed. Past the laundry room, he stood on his tiptoes at the workbench to reach the clamp light.

He'd already laid newspaper around his old schoolhouse desk, having wanted to begin last night after Scouts. "Always cut away from yourself,"

Scoutmaster had said. Blaise hadn't understood what that meant. But when Scoutmaster demonstrated, with long strokes so that the shaving curled like a rind, Blaise knew this was for safety. Last night, Blaise had slept with the red pocket knife under his pillow.

Sitting at his desk, he examined the flowing grain of his block, looking for knots—for problems. It was a good block. Blaise extended the thin silver knife. He carved one corner, then another, rounding the edges and improving the aerodynamics. For Blaise, the racer already existed in the wood. His task was to release it. The block was almost a car when an earthquake interrupted the steady process of carving.

The concrete floor cracked. Powder spewed from the fractures and dust fell through the slatted ceiling. The clamp light shifted, elongating shadows. Blaise sneezed and sneezed again. Then he resumed carving, drawing the racer from his mind. His palm swelled and the muscle between his thumb and forefinger bulged. Dad called down the stairs. Blaise was about go to up, but the door slammed shut. Above, something growled and scratched on the living room's hardwood floor. Mom and Sister screamed—it reminded Blaise of the time he sprayed Sister with the hose on her birthday. Any other day and he wouldn't have been punished.

Lastly, he heard three gunshots and then no more screaming, but through this Blaise kept his concentration.

When his carving hand was too sore, he switched and carved just as deftly with his other hand. But with each stroke the racer was more real, so the stakes became higher. A drop of sweat ran down his cheek. Blaise polished the axles with steel wool and he knew to apply graphite lube before competition. He spent a great deal of concentration on polishing. Happily, Blaise discovered sanding to be as simple as petting the cat.

And yet, the final touch—the racing stripe—loomed in his mind.

It must be straight, he thought.

Blaise glanced at his bottles of craft paint on the workbench. Blue had fallen on its side and rolled. When he stood to grab it, an explosion from the laundry room pushed him into the workbench. Concrete pebbles and wood splinters struck him. Fire bloomed in the doorway. The heat burned his hair and his skin, filling his nostrils with a caustic stench. A frequency rose to a high pitch in his ears, then silence reprieved his anxiety, like muting a scary movie.

Blaise moved his jaw side to side, then grabbed his racer and stuffed his hoodie pouch with his paints and brush. As he passed the laundry room he peered through smoke and saw a black meteorite. It looked like scrap iron corroded by acid. He'd seen one at the science museum just like it. Blaise leapt over the impact crater. He ran up the stairs counting to thirteen faster than he'd ever done. Slamming the door, he nearly caught his racer in the jamb.

In the living room, Blaise smelled fresh air mixing with fumes. Creeping to the edge of the meteorite hole, he leaned and peered up through the busted roof into dark ruffled clouds. Blaise leaned out farther to see an angel in full plumage carrying Dad and Mom, and Sister hung from Mom's skirt holding an umbrella with the cat sitting proudly inside.

Like a kite with bows on the string, Blaise thought, waving goodbye.

His hearing returned when he opened the front door, which sucked open and exhaled closed. The air was heavy. Wavy heat lines obscured Blaise's vision. In the cul-de-sac, neighborhood dogs played with walking human corpses, barking and snatching rotten limbs, running off to gnaw them.

Other Cubs had named their racers: *Cheetah Speeder, Burnin' Blubber, Snot Wheels.* Blaise could not think of a name. The winner of the derby won a special merit badge.

Blaise was afraid of dogs, but his desire to get to the church community center was stronger. He ran to the sidewalk and crept along his neighbor's high hedge. The hedge trembled and Blaise sprinted away as a band of zoo gorillas burst through it. He saw they were headed for the water tower on the hill behind the houses. Squinting through the haze, he saw many people dressed in white gathered there.

As he ran, a steady clack on the sidewalk grew underneath his feet. His sneaker had come untied. He dropped to one knee in the grass and tied the knot, then doubled it for safety. Thinking on it, he switched knees and doubled the other knot. Blaise stood still for a moment watching the matted grass lift back up. Above, the sky swirled with rust and slate-colored clouds. A dark feeling overtook him.

No more blue sky, he thought.

From the end of his street, Blaise looked down the sledding hill toward the brick library. Behind the library, the white church steeple pointed at a thousand birds in murmuration. The shaking earth tripped him, and he rolled down the hill. Blaise dropped his racer and knocked his head on the ground. Dizzy, he steadied himself on his hands and knees. He checked his hoodie's contents, crawled to his racer, and ran a wobbly line through the park. All the tree shadows were cast in the wrong places.

The library stood nearly undisturbed; its dark windows reflected

Main Street's jigsawed and burning store fronts. The library doors were locked, but a Bible-sized hole in one window invited Blaise to hurl chunks of broken road until the hole was large enough to crawl through. Glass shards chimed under his sneakers and the library smelled like old books. He crept under a librarian's desk near a flickering strip light to paint his racer.

Hurry! Blaise thought. His head felt heavy.

The blue paint dried fast, but it didn't look right. Another coat was closer, but his mental image demanded one more. Three coats gave the correct sheen. Blaise tried to steady his hand for the racing stripe, but it would not stop shaking. A hollow creaking noise steadily amplified throughout the room. The light zapped out. The desk jumped and the shelves disgorged their books. Blaise covered his ears.

He pulled his undershirt over his nose and washed his brush with his sweat. Then he swirled the brush tip on the bottle's rim, working the paint in and making a point. Rotating the racer horizontally, he brought the brush to meet it. With vise-like concentration, Blaise painted the racing stripe—just as he'd painted it in his mind days before. But it wasn't right. Blaise again dipped his brush, worked it into a finer point and traced the stripe.

Now he knew it was perfect. He had found the flaw and straightened it.

But an aftershock knocked the brush into the racer's hood. Blaise's eyes ballooned. He held his breath. Gently, he rubbed at the smudge with his hoodie's sleeve and it came off. Lying on his back, Blaise clutched the racer to his chest and exhaled. The carpet felt like toothbrush bristles.

With his racer completed, Blaise ran outside, along the blown out walls of dental and attorney offices, to the churchyard. Atop the steeple, a barefoot man perched. He wore white cloth and hoisted a flaming sword. Something like a censer dangled from his other hand. Beneath him, the heavy front doors opened a crack. Heads peered out, and then arms reached to drag Blaise inside. He tilted his head a moment and then dashed away across the grass to the community center.

When Blaise turned the doorknob, the barefoot man lowered his blade like the long hand of a clock.

Blaise pressed his palm to the wall and found the light switch. He saw the racetrack mounted on a table and swooping down to the floor. The floor was blanketed with white ceiling tile dust that reminded Blaise of snow. He puffed his lungs and blew the dust off the track. He coughed and dripped sweat. Then Blaise held his racer before his eyes, spun it once to enjoy it from every angle, and placed it on the start line.

Only his fingertips kept the racer from going. Reluctantly, Blaise released it.

It flew smoothly down the track, across the floor and into the bathroom, where it clanged against a porcelain tile. He gasped. There wasn't enough air anymore to fill his lungs. The community center door creaked open. The barefoot man entered, carrying his sword. His other hand held a long strand of twine, and from the twine hung a well-crafted birdhouse. His somber gaze fell upon Blaise.

Blaise smiled.

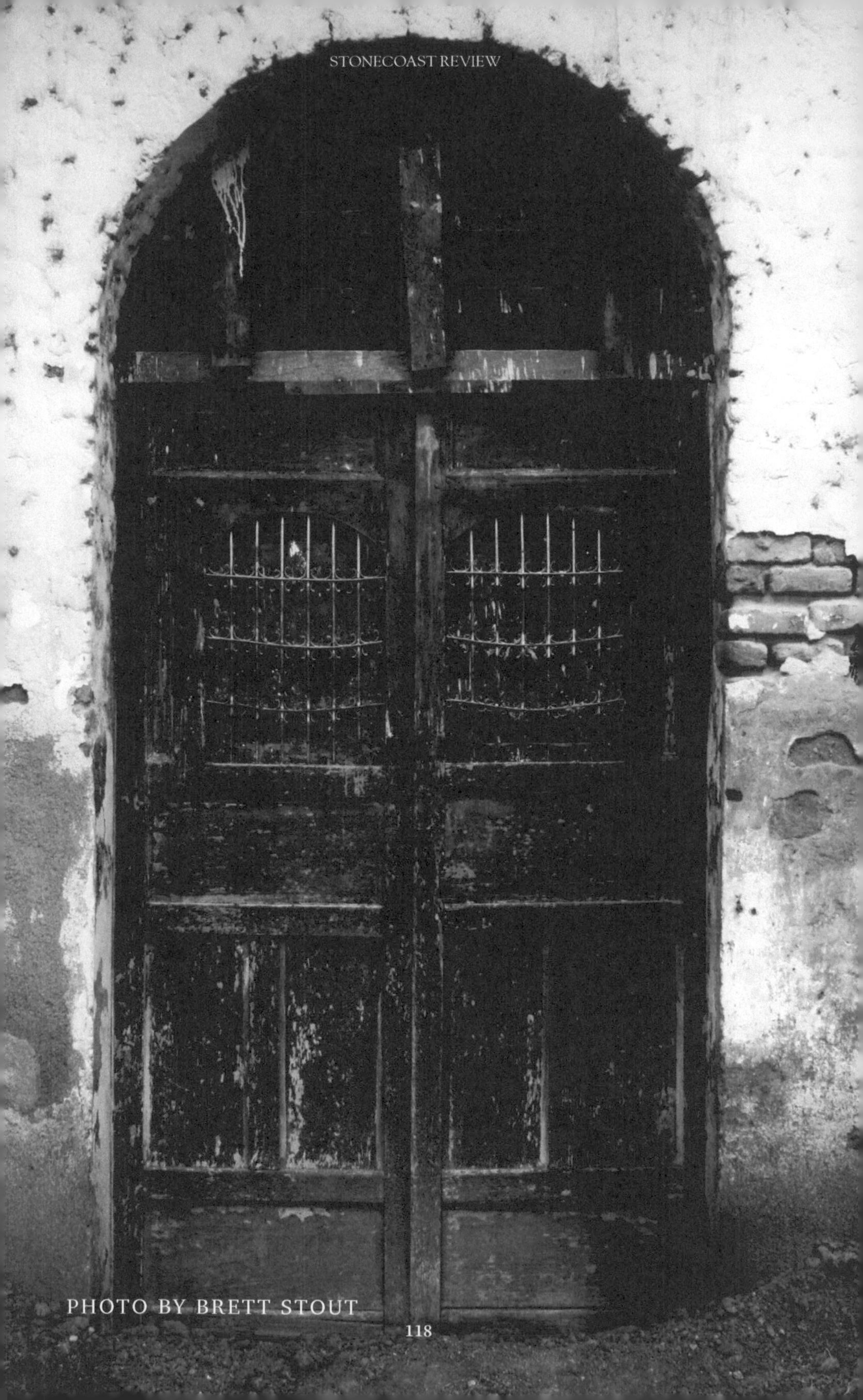

PHOTO BY BRETT STOUT

Judith Lichtendorf

The Rubber Bands are Back

Bereavement groups are a clever concept. It's been three months, four months—enough. Your friends and family don't want to listen anymore, they want you to cheer up, move on. That's the phrase: "it's time to move on." But for a lot of us, it's not. Hence the bereavement group, a weekly date with people who, just like you, want to talk about dead husbands, or wives. Usually the group is all women.

Except now, this group has Frank. He arrived four weeks ago, and since then it's been very clear there's a man in the room.

Until Frank, we were six oldish widows plus Gladys, the forty-something, razor-thin, always-smiling social worker who leads our sharing sessions. We don't talk here—we share. So before Frank, we've been sharing away, the sadness, the loneliness, the getting-rid-of-the-clothes, the loneliness, the bills, the overwhelming paperwork, the loneliness, whether or not to burden the children, the taxes, the loneliness. Of course, six grieving women all sharing takes some tricky moderating. Gladys is usually good at interrupting someone conducting a monologue, as in, Frieda, thank you, we'll come back to that, but other people are waiting to share.

But since Frank joined it's been like a runaway train—Loretta and Maida telling their stories in detail, stories we women have heard over and over, but Frank hasn't. All the conversation is directed at him. Here's Loretta: Tell me Frank, do you ever talk to your wife? That's what I was doing, talking to Richard when I found the rubber bands...

Great. The rubber bands are back.

I am trying to behave like a caring, sympathetic adult. After all, why hurt her feelings? But it's hard for me to understand Loretta, who is a nice-enough-looking woman, with the exception of her inability to get her lipstick exactly and only on her lips. Still, she seems reasonably intelligent, so for the life of me I don't understand how she can—without embarrassment—not just monopolize the conversation, but tell the same stupid story, using the same words, in the same sequence. The rubber bands. The closet. The sister-in-law from the first marriage.

In my secret heart I'm saying, to use my second mother-in-law's phrase, "please god give me strength."

It's simply unfair—we only have an hour. My time to talk about myself and my grief, my issues, is being depleted while this seventy-five year old woman talks about the rubber bands. I want to tell the group about Louis—how gleeful he was on his deathbed. And yes, I know they've heard it before, but still, I want to tell them about it again. And it's not just me—there are all the others in the group. We're all sitting, thinking our thoughts, waiting for our turn to talk. I mean share.

It's "share." We're waiting to share.

But Loretta keeps going.

And there they were, she says. Just lying on the floor of the closet. I mean, Frank, there had to be at least fifty of them. All sizes, all colors, and there was no way they could have gotten there. I was amazed, Frank. Totally amazed. I mean, it was eerie...

Why doesn't Gladys control Loretta, let another person share?

After Joe, my second husband, died, I felt I didn't need a bereavement group. I knew Joe was dying, Joe knew he was dying—it's over, I'm fine, nothing to talk about, just let me get on with my life. Ten months later, standing in front of an Italian restaurant on Second Avenue, a place Joe and I loved, I was wailing away like a lost child on a crowded beach. So much for "just get on with my life."

I joined a group and it worked. I had a safe place to cry, and tell the story of Joe's death, again and again and again. All the members liked hearing it, and I liked hearing their deaths. Like a book club, but different. After my third husband Louis died, for the last six months on Monday afternoons, I've been going to my community center and sharing with the gang.

We meet in the conference room. It's a big room, with a pull down screen for PowerPoint meetings, slick tables arranged in a circle with slick chairs with thin legs that stick in the slick carpet—perfect for younger people who attend PowerPoint meetings, but three months ago poor Gail—arthritic, walks-with-a-cane Gail—tried to stand up, but her chair legs stuck and she fell and bruised her left cheekbone, her left elbow, and her hip. Gladys wanted to call 911, but Gail insisted she was okay, and she was—black and blue and sore for a few weeks, that's all.

Now we're all careful when we stand up and make sure our chairs aren't stuck. And speaking of careful, in this post-Frank era, Loretta is more carefully dressed. Today it's a black silk shirt, tight white pants and white kitten heels. Pearls. Her hair is freshly blonded and shaped to curve around her face. Of course, there's still that lipstick issue.

So Frank, Loretta says, god is my witness, I couldn't believe it, but there they were again! Maybe fifty of them, different colors, different sizes just lying on the floor of our bedroom closet. And I don't keep rubber bands in the bedroom—I have them in the kitchen, on a doorknob…

I'm thinking about Louis, about his own unique count-down at the end. His birthday was May 16, and the date, one day before he died, was November 16. Louis spent his life on Wall Street crunching numbers—and the relevant numbers were these: my second husband died at seventy-two, and poor Alex, my first, at sixty-seven.

I was in the visitor's chair with Louis in his cordoned off hospital room, the area where the most gravely ill are tended. Or herded. Louis was resting, flaccid white skin, breathing shallow. It's so hard to die. With a grunt, Louis slowly pushed himself up and removed the oxygen mask, holding it up like a microphone.

I have something to say, he said.

A weak voice, but he was smiling. Okay, kiddo, I said. Go for it.

My dear wife, Louis said, I am happy to inform you that as of today, I, your number three, have turned seventy-four and a half! Louis paused for breath. And—Hah!—that makes me your oldest husband. Hah! I have lived longer than all of them. Seventy-four and a half. Hah! Hah!

He gave me his biggest grin, (you can imagine Louis at eight years old, a proud little kid who's gotten a gold star on his math test). Then with just a little bit of a groan, he lay slowly back down on his pillow and put the oxygen mask back on. Yes, he was dying, but still. Louis was triumphant. He had done it. Seventy-four and a half.

He was smiling as he drifted back to sleep.

I want to tell this to the group.

And Frank, Loretta says, this was the second time. And when I told my sister-in-law Margie, well, she's not really my sister-in-law, she's my divorced husband's sister (right, we know that, Loretta) but she says I'll always be her sister-in-law, (right, you've said that and said that, Loretta). Anyhow, when I told Margie about it she said, of course it's Richard, he wants you to know he's watching you. And I said, oh Margie, do you really think so? And she said, what else could it be? He's sending you a message. And that's what I've started to think, maybe Richard is there, somewhere, still watching over me...

Loretta starts to cry. We all wait.

Our leader, Gladys, says in a soft voice, this is very hard for you, isn't it?

Yes, Loretta says, I'm sorry.

I reach into my handbag and pull out a pack of tissues and push them over to Loretta. She blows her nose. The conversation starts again.

Maida: Well, Frank, I don't know if you feel this way, but I know John is with me, I actually feel him watching me, I even talk to him. Just last night I was talking to him—who gave you permission to leave, you big lug? That's exactly what I said to him.

She crosses her right leg and swings it back and forth. She, too, is carefully dressed, plus she's done eyeliner and blush. She's got a blue t-shirt with "Grandma Power" in sequins, and a matching blue skirt. She switches legs, swings her left one back and forth. Frank? She says.

Frank sighs. He's a big man, six feet tall, overweight. He's eighty, almost bald; he was married for fifty-five years. For the last three, his wife had ovarian cancer, and finally died two months ago. He says, I guess I don't feel like that. Maybe it's a man-woman thing, but I—I know she's gone. I know I'm alone. Everything hurts, wherever I look I see her stuff, her pillow on the couch, her makeup in the bathroom—excuse me, sorry. He controls himself. But no, I don't believe that spooky stuff. Lucy is dead. She's gone. I don't have her anymore.

Loretta says, but what about the rubber bands? How do you explain the rubber bands?

I can't stop myself.

Loretta, I say, if Richard is really there why doesn't he leave you a note? Or a flower? Why is he communicating by throwing rubber bands on your closet floor? It doesn't make sense.

Gladys is always diplomatic at times like this. Well, this is very interesting, she says. Do the rest of you feel like your departed loved one is still somehow around and watching you?

Loretta is one of the "he just dropped dead." Her husband went off to buy two bagels for a breakfast treat. A morning like every other, except she got a phone call—Richard dropped dead in the bagel store. She rushed to the hospital, but he had been declared. The other "just dropped deads" are Maida and Gail—Maida's husband was sitting at the computer, and stood up, perhaps to answer the phone hanging on a wall nearby, stumbled, cut his head on the desk edge, concussed, and since he took blood thinners, he bled out.

I was having dinner, with a woman I don't even like, Maida keeps telling Frank. And the food was awful and I spent thirty-seven dollars including tip—and while I'm eating, Jerry's lying there. By the time I got home, there was nothing I could do. I guess this is very different than your experience, Frank, Maida says. After all, you and Lucy knew the end was coming. But for me, it was a total shock.

She smiles at him—a big smile that shows her upper and lower teeth, all of them ringed in black. They're capped; a cosmetic intervention that happened years ago; now Maida's gums are retreating. Frank is wiping his eyes.

Frank, do you want to say something to Maida? Gladys asks.

Frank shakes his head, no.

Maida says, oh Frank, I know how hard this is.

Oh yes, Loretta says, oh it's very hard, Frank. It's very sad, very hard. We all know what you're feeling, you're among friends and supporters. I'm here for you, Frank.

Gail is the other "just dropped dead." Her husband, Harry, knew he had cardiac disease. He saw specialist after specialist, was given options—and for whatever reason refused to do anything. Gail keeps asking the group, what could she do? What could she do?

Frank says, I don't know how I'm going to live. I don't know how I can keep going without Lucy. All I want to do is cry.

Oh Frank, Maida says. Oh Frank, I understand, I know what you're going through.

Yes, Loretta says, I know what you're feeling.

Frank says, I don't know how you women do it.

Two other women spent years with husbands in slow decay. Three if you count me. Sylvia's husband fell down a flight of stairs, hit his head, and his brain was never exactly the same. He could just about follow a PG-13 movie plot. As the years went by, he developed what she describes as "a little dementia."

Frieda's husband had bladder cancer. It was treated, went into remission, a few years passed, it came back, he grew weak, they took one final cruise, and then he died. I was sitting by his bed in the hospital, Frieda said. Those machines, monitors, you know, beep beep beep, they were slowing down, I knew he was going, and the thing is, he had that big oxygen mask and the tube down his throat, and tape all over his face—there wasn't any room. I couldn't even kiss him to say goodbye.

I'm the only one with three dead husbands. My first two died of cancer, and number three, poor Louis, died of everything. Name it, he had it.

Frank clears his throat. It's quiet—Frank is going to speak. There's a respectful hush—this time he's speaking to me. I hope this isn't rude, he says, I hope it's okay to ask. But I just keep wondering, which husband do you miss the most?

Oh, goodness, I say, Oh, it's fine to ask. It's just that I've never thought about it that way. I guess my best answer is—I miss them all. If one of them could come back—any one of them, I would be incredibly happy. If all of them came back it would be a very strange cocktail party.

I think it is a funny answer, but it seems no one else does.

They wait.

I guess I miss Louis the most, I finally say. There's something to that song, 'When I'm not near the one I love, I love the one I'm near…' I mean, Louis is my most recent husband, so he's the one who's absence I'm most aware of—but I loved them all. I mean, I married them. They were all my favorites.

Gladys says, oh, that was beautiful, thank you for sharing that with us.

I want to tell them of his last day. I got to the hospital, chatted with the nurse who told me we had a good night.

We.

Louis was lying on his back, peaceful, sleeping, until suddenly he convulsed, shaking the bed, his entire body in wild motion, I'm screaming help, we need help here, and people came running to his curtained space and as suddenly as they began, the convulsions stopped. In the shocked silence Louis looked up at me blankly and said:

was I really flying?

But we only have five more minutes. And Maida is talking on and on about her mother who preferred Maida's brother, he was the one who went to college, but she was sent to secretarial school.

Just because I was a girl, Maida is saying, and girls don't matter, that's what it was about for my mother…

Those were Louis' last words: was I really flying?

I love that he thought he was flying.

I hope that was how he felt—that he wasn't afraid, that he wasn't scared, that he was flying. What do I do with this thought?

I want to share it with the group.

I'm afraid our time is up, Gladys says. This was a very productive session. And I look forward to seeing all of you next week. Now, remember, be careful of those chairs everyone.

Does anyone want to go for coffee? Loretta says. Frank?

ART BY DAVID SUCH

Kaely Horton

Tell Me You're All Right

So first there was the summer you didn't sleep, she says, and then there was the day I found red lines on your wrist, and then there was the time you disappeared for two months, and when's it going to end, Jenny, when don't I have to worry about you anymore? We are perched on tall stools in the corner coffeeshop, nursing beverages that threaten to spill—Alison's a creamy London Fog, mine a tall latte with tiny white clovers swirled against the brown. I tip my mug sideways to disrupt the designs, pretending to consider her question. It doesn't seem wise to promise anything right now.

And you shouldn't be drinking coffee, she adds.

I resolve to quit telling Alison about my medication schedule. A couple of WebMD searches and suddenly she thinks she's my personal health coach. She hunches across from me on the stool, her gnarled black braids stiff on either shoulder. Her blue eyes fix to my face and dart away, fix to my face and dart away, until I feel like I'm in the company of a couple of concerned moths. Her hands grip the mug as if she expects me to take it away from her.

Maybe you should just lie to me, she says. Tell me you're all right. That's what you do with everyone else.

It's true. As far as most of my friends are concerned, I spent last summer backpacking in the Uintas. Only Alison knew enough to connect the dots. Alison, who knows summers are bad for me. She fought through my deflections with alarming ease, pounding on my door at one o'clock in the morning because she really wanted me to know *right then* that she loved me, and oh, by the way, completely unrelated, where was the box of pills, and could she have it, please?

I shouldn't have agreed to meet her today. I feel a sinking in my stomach as I follow the broken green curve of the fern in the corner, avoiding Alison's eyes. Some part of me wishes I could back up our friendship to the time when she knew nothing about my brain chemistry, when all our conversations revolved around which *Doctor Who* companion we wanted to travel with, but she knows too much now. Her fear is the uninvited third guest each time I see her, hanging in the background of every movie marathon, every lake hike, every coffee date.

She stares at me, her eyes expectant, her toes curled around the stool rung as her sandals hang off her heels.

It's the middle of June, she says.

So?

I see Alison's chest rise and fall. She is marshalling strength. I think of all the things she could say next. Summers are bad for you, she will say. You know summers are always bad. Do you have a therapist, and how many? Group therapy or solo? Are you still on Lexapro, and are you still not sleeping? Are you taking walks? Are you talking to people? Did you tell them at work? Do you have pills in your house? Should you?

An orange ladybug with a crushed wing limps across the table. I can see its tiny legs clinging to the wood.

Should we kill it? I ask.

Alison glances down, distracted.

I don't know. It's still walking.

The bug's black limbs flail for purchase. The surface of the table is too smooth. It strains sideways, off-balance, and I wonder what must have happened to get a ladybug into that state.

Do you remember the day we went fishing? Alison says. There is a softness in her expression as she watches the ladybug, a recognition.

Fishing?

We were something like five. We caught a shit ton of bugs—maybe they were ladybugs—and put them in your mom's colander and marched them outside to the rain gutter and just sat there forever drowning all the bugs. We never caught any fish.

Shocking.

Why did we think there were fish in the rain gutters?

I don't know. It must have made sense at the time.

I pull my crumpled white napkin in front of the ladybug, offering a path up to the windowsill.

Careful, Alison says, the orange ones bite.

A momentary fluttering, legs like wisps of thread beneath the stocky bright body, and then a stillness, a relief, as the legs find a soft place to land. The bug stands for a moment, the napkin giving beneath its weight, and begins to climb.

Alison's eyes follow the ladybug up the windowsill. A few strands of her left braid are coming undone, tiny rebels against the glossy grain.

I want gelato, I say.

Alison looks up. I know that it's not just the prospect of creamy raspberry bringing life into her eyes. I understand, with a throbbing recognition, that there is something refreshing about hearing me want something. She'll take anything, the tiniest expression of pleasure or desire, the barest thread of belonging to and in the world. Maybe we both will.

Yeah, she says. Yeah, that sounds good. Gelato.

We disappear from the coffee shop with a scraping of stools. The orange ladybug scrabbles across the windowsill, its crushed wing trembling. We leave it suspended, caught in a vortex of fate and time. Maybe it crawls interminably and dies, or maybe it finds its way eventually to the corner fern. I will wonder about it later as the summer progresses, as the heat closes in, as I get out of bed or I don't, as Alison calls and I answer, as I don't answer, as I peel away mornings like scabs. For months afterward, I will wonder if the ladybug survived. The answer will never satisfy me.

PHOTO BY MARIA GREEN

PHOTO BY JEFFREY ALFIER

William O'Heaney

I Do Like to Drink

I like to drink.

Or to be more precise, I have a great attachment to the pleasures of drinking. I love bars. I love the promise of the gleaming rows of multicolored bottles that line the back. I love the feeling of a heavy rocks glass in my hand filled with ice cubes and an amber liquid. I love the warmth that first drink generates up the back of my neck to my cerebellum. I love the pull from the neck of a pint bottle outdoors on a chilly day, and I love the warm glow that wraps around me like a favorite blanket once the alcohol takes hold.

I grew up in a drinking culture, which one doesn't matter—a neighborhood enclave with customs, rites, and rules. Any life event that engendered strong emotions was bathed in alcohol. Drinking was woven into the fabric of family and community, and if there were rumors of a member of our tribe who had problems with alcohol, well, that's something we didn't talk about. Pleasure and happiness generated by alcohol is unfortunately fleeting. What was once magical becomes repetitive and pathetic. What was funny and high-spirited at twenty years old is sad at forty.

I'll spare the drunkalog and messy details. After a long series of successes and setbacks, I finally have what medical professionals refer to as "long-term sustained recovery." Fourteen years sober.

I miss drinking almost everyday. When I hear the clink of ice filling a tall glass I feel a shiver race up my spine. An aroma, a spoken phrase, any memory can bring back old urges.

Sobriety is not a struggle; I cannot imagine a scenario where I would be tempted to take a drink. My life is full and rich, and I won't risk complication. I stay vigilant on a daily basis, and remind myself "today isn't a good day to drink."

But . . . I do like to drink.

Helen Waters

When I Was a Front for a Drug Trafficker

When I was in middle school, my mom had a job at Jovita's, a restaurant and music venue in South Austin. She did a few things for the business, including cleaning, managing the wait staff, and booking shows or doing the sound for concerts, all so she could play her songs there sometimes.

Her boss was a man named Mayo, and he owned Jovita's and the property behind it, where he had a large house, a compound of sorts.I only saw his house from outside, but I spent time at the restaurant with my mom and saw him there. I remember the restaurant's entire backyard and the path to the house all being covered in military-style, camouflage jungle netting.

I'm not sure how it happened, but my mom and I started hanging out with Mayo outside of the restaurant. I remember two outings in detail. One time we all drove to McKinney Falls State Park on the edge of town, where Mayo said we would accompany him on his daily exercise walk. While we were on the walk, he told me that there was four thousand dollars in cash in his trunk that wouldn't be there when we got back. I told this to my mom later, and she said he'd just been messing around with me, kidding me.

The other outing I remember was a trip to Corpus Christi. It was a three-hour drive from Austin. It was just like before. We parked the car in a public lot by the beach and went for a walk. We walked to a shopping center where Mayo bought me an outfit: Army-green cargo shorts and a red tank top with a dragon. I think I wore the new clothes out of the store because we went to dinner at a kind of fancy restaurant that was built over the water, and I remember feeling underdressed in my shorts. After that, we walked back to the car and drove back to Austin. We couldn't have been in Corpus for more than two hours.

I remember bringing up these trips to my mom several times as I got older, and each time she would beg me to forget about them, reminding me that Mayo had been convicted of murder. Twice. Especially when I started writing, and I would bring up wanting to use that time in my life for a story, my mother would cry and plead with me to keep it to myself. She told me people would come after me, would kill me, if I wrote those stories. It was so hard for me to take her seriously, but I did as she asked, until now. Mayo died two years ago, just before he was about to go to trial for being the leader of a huge heroin-selling operation.

I told my mom about finally writing this, and she said it doesn't matter if Mayo is dead, that he still has people out there, and she said, again, that they would find me and kill me. So I said, "Fine, Mom, then I'll die."

Oonagh Doherty

Diasporas

Anita's stepfather died, she's sitting *shiva*
and so at group we raised our cups.
Death is what you drink to, what you write to;
like passion it will wipe slates clean.

Isn't it funny—Boricua or Jew
we light the candles.
Clocks stop for small shrines, temporary.

As I write, yellow jacket walks on paper's edge,
tiger abdomen softer than I thought.
She taps black feelers, stretches, says,
this substance is strange, yet it is mine.

I think of Anita, a Jewish poet with a Yale doctorate
teaching writing to Taino dropouts in Holyoke.
Perhaps the culture graft is not so odd.

Consider Old Man Epstein of the furniture store:
at eighty how he shook
and pounded on the doors demanding rent.
He was sometimes good for a wreath
for the constant wakes at *Puerta del Cielo*.
The personal touch, his rage, the tenants understood it.
El Viejo, they said, every mouth curved with the private joke.

A ghetto boy today, cycling past—
by the Jewish cemetery he crossed himself.
I thought *that was for Anita that was sent*.
Sometimes with all our errors, we recognize.

PHOTO BY MARIA GREEN

PHOTO BY BRETT STOUT

Orlan Roe Owen

Consider Moments

Consider moments
on which we balance our lives:

In this suspended time of growing light,
    a wakening to sound and movement,

    I separate rind and pith
    from grapefruit sections,

    listen to repeated calls
    of mourning doves,

    answers folded in leaves
    by yesterday's breeze.

Deer Crossing

Tonight deer graze
May grass

at the highway's edge,
ghosts in my headlights,

only half a shade
lighter than the dark

eyes like a constellation
with no name.

PHOTO BY MARIA GREEN

ART BY CARL ERICKSON

Mendigas

I walk around the *zocalo*
to avoid the press
of shawl-draped women
who tug at my sleeve
palms upturned.

Ahead *mariachis* flank
cathedral steps
and begin to play
as a wedding party bursts out.

Guests throw rice nonstop
as the couple descends the steps,
followed by a tall cake on a platform
supported by poles borne by four men.
Quickly they load the line of stretch limos
and drive off.

The shawled women
move onto the steps, crouch or kneel.

I watch
as the woman closest to me
brushes with long, thin fingers,
and flicks the grains from the wide joints
of the tile-paved steps
into a small white cone.

I watch
till my stare becomes uncomfortable.

Lee Kahrs

Getting to Know You

O nce a month for three to five days over the past forty years, I am reminded I have a uterus. The other twenty-five days of the month, I forget that I am a woman and stroll through my life straddling that line between male and female. I think of myself as a "spork." I'm not transgender, but as a butch lesbian, I am very male-identified—in my walk, demeanor and wardrobe, but also in my sensibility—so much so that the only other time I think of myself as a woman is when my legal name is used for medical billing purposes or debt collection.

No, I am not telling you my real name.

O.K., it's "Lisa."

Ugh. It's hard to type.

That is not my name, but the one given to me by my parents in April 1966, when it was the nation's most popular name for girls. I went through school with at least four other Lisas.

When I was eighteen, however, I viewed attending college in another state as an opportunity to start fresh with a new name, and I started calling myself "Lee." It was nice and short and androgynous, and everyone I've met since then knows me as Lee. I was coming out and terrified, but at least I had a name I chose that fit me and who I was becoming.

But every twenty-five days since the fifth grade, my menstrual cycle reminds me that I am a woman and have female body parts. As I turned fifty-two, menopause was within reach when my uterus placed itself front and center in my day-to-day consciousness. It was the start of summer when I had incredible cramping pain during the first part of my period. It felt like I was being knifed in the gut. An ultrasound confirmed four fibroid tumors. That's when I really began, for the first time in my life, to have a relationship with my womb.

I was actually kind of impressed with the exploitation of my otherwise unused organ—I had been an empty vessel for fifty years, so why wouldn't some benign fibroid tumors take up residence there? And here I thought I was having either constipation, appendicitis, or perhaps gall bladder trouble. It *never* occurred to me that the intense pain I felt in my gut would be because of a problem with my woman parts. In my mind, my uterus was very much like an appendix, a rather useless thing that only exists to fill space.

Before the first ultrasound, I was in the gynecologist's office in South Burlington, filling out forms and answering questions about cancer history in my family, as well as some very personal questions about my sex life.

"Are you sexually active?" asked the young, bespectacled physician's assistant.

"Uh, yes."

"Great!" she said, and I smirked.

"Yay!" I said raising my fist. "Yay for sex!"

"Is there any chance you could be pregnant?" she asked.

I choked on my own spit.

"Uh, no, absolutely one hundred percent *zero* chance of that," I said flatly.

Then the doctor arrived, a strawberry-blond woman named Jane Connolly. She was perhaps thirty-five and five foot nothing. I liked her immediately. She told me her theory: that a burst ovarian cyst had led to the pain and was concrete evidence of fibroid tumors in my uterus. Then I took off my pants and we started the ultrasound. She squeezed lime green gel on the end of what looked like a dildo, and asked me if I was ready.

"Sure," I said. "Now, if you find a baby in there, it'll be a medical miracle. We'll be famous!"

"I'll be sure to call the papers," she said with a smile.

And then she went in. I leaned back and tried to relax. Over my head, tacked to the ceiling tiles, was a mobile made out of small sticks of driftwood with seashells dangling from them. It was cheesy, but at least it was something to look at as someone I had just met went into a place not often entered. I could only see the side of the monitor with the image of my uterus, but it reminded me of the ultrasound photos of my granddaughter in utero tacked on the fridge at home.

"Hey, can I get a print out of the ultrasound of the fibroids?" I asked. "I can put them on my fridge with the ones of my granddaughter."

Dr. Connolly looked at me out of the corner of her eye.

"Fibroids aren't nearly as cute as a baby," she said drily.

"I know," I said, "but you have to admit this technology is pretty amazing."

She kept rooting around, past the point where I was comfortable with the situation, but I had to stay put. I just kept staring at that godforsaken mobile.

"I can't seem to find your ovaries," Dr. Connolly announced.

"Well, it's dark in there," I said.

She laughed and pulled out.

"Well, if I can't find them, it's actually good because that means they are small and not inflamed, so I'm not concerned."

I was of no help, since I had no idea where my ovaries were either. It should come as no surprise that my knowledge of female anatomy is, at best, weak—even for a lesbian. I know where the clitoris is, and I guess that's all I really thought I needed to know. My wife, who is a nurse, drew me a diagram when I was first diagnosed.

Let me be clear here when I say that my relationship with my female body is dysmorphic and unconventional, and that I recognize that millions of women, straight and gay alike, love and celebrate their female bodies. They are as comfortable with their periods as I am splitting wood, which is to say, it is a part of them. And if they have children, their uterus is a precious and revered part of who they are. When those women have to have a hysterectomy, it is very traumatic. They say they feel like "less of a woman." And when those same women go through menopause, it ushers in a period of grieving.

I have never wrestled in that tournament.

I don't know what it feels like to want to bear children, and I don't know what it feels like to give birth. There was no ticking biological clock once I hit my twenties and thirties, no deep-seated desire to create life and bear it. By the time I hit thirty-five, my deepest desire was for a twelve-pack and a fishing boat.

An MRI a few weeks later dispelled the initial diagnosis. I didn't have four fibroid tumors. I had *fourteen*. It turned out I had a variety-pack of fibroids, a little something for everyone. I had a large, six-centimeter fibroid adhered to my uterine wall, and another one attached by a stalk to my uterus, like a leaf on a tree. I had small fibroids and large fibroids, the mother of them all sitting directly on my cervix, like a beefy doorman at an exclusive dance club.

I had an interventional radiology (IR) procedure in November, where the radiologists went into the femoral artery in my leg and shot tiny plastic pieces into the veins and arteries feeding the uterus, blocking the blood supply. In theory, this shrinks the fibroids. Everything was fine for three months.

I came home from work on Valentine's Day, put the mail on the kitchen table, let the dogs out, and made a beeline for the bathroom. As I was peeing, I felt something coming out of me that should not have been coming out of me. I wiped, stood up and turned to see a toilet bowl full of blood. I put in a super tampon, but minutes later I felt that leaking feeling and headed back to the bathroom. I pulled out the tampon, which was soaked through, and a torrent of blood and blood clots came out into the toilet. The tampon had been in for less than four minutes.

I called my gynecologist from my seated position on the toilet as more blood and clots came out. It felt like globs of Jell-O exiting my vagina.

I didn't know they were blood clots until the nurse told me on the phone.

"We're going to call in a prescription for progesterone for you," she said. "Can you get to the pharmacy?"

"Yes," I said as larger Jell-O pieces came splashing into the toilet.

"Take it as prescribed for the first few days," the nurse continued. "You will need to rest this afternoon and do as little as possible. You'll feel weak."

No kidding.

I was in the middle of my own Valentine's Day Massacre. I'm not squeamish, but I had never seen so much of my own blood in one place. It was like the final scene in the movie *Carrie*. When I got home from the pharmacy, I changed my underwear again, popped a progesterone, put in a Super Plus tampon and waited for the massacre to ease up. It took about three hours for the hormones to kick in.

It turns out the IR was unsuccessful. Those fourteen fibroids weren't going quietly.

"We have to do a biopsy," Dr. Connolly said when I saw her again.

We tried to do it right there in her office, but the doorman fibroid was having none of it. The doctor could not get into my uterus to get the tissue for the biopsy. Then she said we'd have to schedule an appointment at the hospital in the operating room. They'd have to put me under in order to get the biopsy done. That's when I called it.

"I think we're working too hard to keep something I have no connection to," I said. "Let's just take the fucker out."

And then a sob got caught in my throat.

I started bawling, right there in the office. My wife Sarah had left me just six days earlier, and the enormity of it all just exploded out of me. I shook with sobs as Dr. Connolly and the surgeon, Dr. Kym Boyman, stood on each side of me, each with a hand on one of my shoulders, as I let it all out. They both looked genuinely concerned.

"That's a lot," Dr. Boyman said.

I nodded and took the tissue offered to me and blew my nose. I wasn't just upset about my marriage ending. In the moment after I made the decision to have a hysterectomy, the one tiny fledgling girl part of me, still left deep inside, mourned.

Either that, or the surgery, on top of divorce, on top of life, was overwhelming me.

For a hot minute. And then it was over. It was like letting a burst of air out of a too-full balloon—just enough to ease the pressure so it doesn't break.

The hysterectomy was scheduled for just over a month later. I continued to live at the house with the animals, and Sarah got a sublet in the next town, close to the hospital where she worked as a birthing center administrator. In planning my month-long leave of absence from work, my doctors needed assurance that there was someone to drive me home after the surgery and stay with me, at least for the first few days. Sarah was the only option, and given her nursing background, a good one, despite our recent development.

She took good care of me. Friends would ask about my recovery and who was with me, and when I told them, they would say, "Huh, how was *that*?" It wasn't as awkward as you might think. After so many years together, Sarah and I are still eminently compatible. I'd had five weeks to process Sarah's leaving by then, and slowly I'd begun to make peace with her decision. My recovery was, frankly, a welcome distraction from the split. We know how to sit together in the living room watching ghost hunting shows and *Roseanne* reruns—Sarah knitting, our dogs laying about.

One night, about four days after the surgery, we were watching TV and something I saw in a commercial prompted me to inform Sarah that I was never getting married again. I expounded on my theory that the institution is a sham, and that humans are sold a bill of goods on the promise of marriage meaning "happily ever after."

She disagreed.

"I think you take the good from every relationship you have," Sarah said, "and you always have that, even if you end up going in different directions."

"Well, that's nice," I said. "I'm not there yet."

"Of course not," she replied. "But hopefully, someday you will be."

She ended up staying for six days, until I could move better and resume dog-walking chores. The night before she went back to her sublet, I bought Sarah dinner at her favorite restaurant to thank her for taking care of me.

Sarah and I will always be in each other's lives, parenting and grandparenting together and separately. My emotions continue to swing from ugly cry to staunch resolve to melancholy to hopefulness—but there is acceptance.

And I am poised to start the next phase of my life, single and uterus-free.

Still, it's a lot.

PHOTO BY MARIA GREEN

Rick Wilber

Today is Today

"You can think of our entire universe, our reality, as one bubble surrounded by an infinite number of other bubbles, each with its own reality. Do those bubbles touch? Can you cross from one to another? That's an entertaining possibility."

Janine Marie Larsen, Ph.D., Physics
University of Loyola at St. Louis

In one tiny part of one of the new bubbles emerging from the bubble that is our particular universe, there is a place and time where you might exist and I might exist where I have a daughter named Janine.

Perhaps, in that tiny bubble, I may have been lucky with sports and found some success. As quarterback in high school, I'll have converted to a tight end in college at the University of Minnesota, where I'll bang heads and block like a demon, catching most of the passes they throw my way. I'll be All Big Twelve, then a second-round draft choice, then I'll make the team in St. Louis for the Brewers and get my chance to start when Rasheed Campbell blows out his left knee. Then I'll never look back. Seven years later I'll wind down my career as a backup on the Falcons, but that will be their Super Bowl year, so I'll get my ring by, mostly, sitting on my butt.

It will be a nice way to spend my twenties. I'll stay single and have a blast, though my body will take a beating. When I lose a couple of steps and the good times come to an end, I'll try to move to broadcasting, but that's a lot harder than you'd think. I won't be able to think that fast on my feet, so it won't work out.

Still, I'll feel like I have plenty of money for life as a grown-up, and you'd think I'd be happy; but it's hard to be a has-been, no matter how much money you've saved. I'll never marry, never have any kids, never grow up, really, and I'll know it. Later in life I'll be lonely and bored and broke. And thanks to all that head-banging work on the offensive line in my football career, I'll literally be losing my mind. Eventually I'll run out of money and run into trouble and only then will I have any regrets.

☙❧

In another tiny part of another emerging bubble where you might exist, I'll break my collarbone in the second game of my senior year of high school, and by the time I'm back the season will be over—my football career along with it. But my left-handed pitching skills will be unfazed by my fractured right clavicle, and I'll pitch us to the state championship where we'll lose by one unearned run. My fastball in the high eighties and my nice, straight change-up will earn me a free ride to Loyola University, where I'll have four good years as a Billiken and five more in the minors before I'll hang them up and get on with real life in the business world.

I'll meet a woman who loves me and I, her. We'll marry and have two sweet kids. I'll have a good life and some nice minor-league memories from Tampa and Atlanta and Durham and Spokane. You'd think I'd be happy.

☙❧

In another tiny part of another of my emerging bubbles where you might exist, the Golden Gophers will keep me at quarterback, and I'll do fine as the starter, though I'll never be a star and I won't make the NFL. I'll knock around a bit in arena football and then swim up to the surface as the quarterback of the Hamilton Tiger Cats. Once, in my nine years there, I'll lead the Ticats to victory in the Grey Cup. In the Canadian Football League there's room to pass and room to run, and I'll do both, often.

I'll meet a woman named Alene in my second season when we'll beat the Alouettes with a lucky rouge. We'll be celebrating at Yancy's on Hanover Street and there she'll be, dark hair and blue eyes, stunning and smart and ambitious. I'll have had a good day on the ground, gaining ninety yards before taking a stinger and coming out of the game. She'll have been there, rooting for the Alouettes, and she'll have seen that hit I took. She'll wonder how I am feeling. Just fine, I'll say, though I'll have a worrisome headache.

She'll be an actor, a successful French Canadian who speaks four languages. I'll feel lucky. By my third season we'll be married. By my fifth season we'll have a child, Janine. We'll call her Jannie.

Janine Marie Larsen will be born two weeks early on July 21st, a Saturday, at four in the morning. Alene will have a rough time of it with a fifteen-hour delivery and then it will only get worse: Jannie's feet, hands, and the epicanthal folds at the eyes all have a certain flaccidity, even for a newborn.

Trisomy 21, the doctor will say.

Down syndrome.

Alene will have been through ultrasound and blood tests and everything will have looked fine. But here will be Jannie, and that will be that. There's a lot these kids can do, the doctor will say as Alene and I both cry. Really, they can accomplish a lot.

Really, the doctor will emphasize.

We'll have a game that night at home, in old Ivor Wynne Stadium against the Alouettes, and Alene will insist I play. So I'll go and do that, earning my paycheck with a couple of touchdown passes and a good enough night of football. I won't remember much of the game. All I'll be able to think about is:

Down syndrome.

I'll go right back to the hospital after the game and Alene will be weak but smiling and more beautiful than ever. There will be a picture the next day in the *Hamilton Spectator* of her with the baby—the whole city will be behind us. I'll hold that baby and kiss her cheek as the cameras whir and click.

Two years will go by when I won't play much: some knee surgery, a discectomy for a herniated disc, a couple more concussions. The docs will say it's time to hang them up and so I will. That's about the time that Alene will get the movie role she's always wanted, filming in Vancouver. Our parting will be amicable. I'll get Jannie and Alene will get visitation rights, and there she'll go, heading west.

I'll have no reason whatsoever to be happy, but, holding Jannie, I will be.

CB ⇛⇝ BD

There is another tiny part of a different bubble where Alene and I will stay together and things will go differently for Jannie. She'll be normal and fussy and hungry at birth, and she won't stop being any of those things right through high school and college. She'll get her brains from her mother, her athleticism from me, and win a full ride to play soccer at Rice, where she'll major in physics. Then she'll choose brawn over brains and turn pro for the Washington Whippets before joining the national team in the Global Cup. She'll be a star and a household name after they beat the French on her hat-trick to win it all.

By that time, I'll be coaching football at Buffalo State and happy enough with how I've reconciled myself to the paycheck and the fall from fame. But Hamilton will treat me well with a big ovation when I go there to see Jannie play a friendly game against the Italians, and she'll have a great day, scoring a brace. We'll have dinner afterward and she'll be polite, but distant, and we'll smile for the cameras and then I'll go my way and she'll go hers.

ᘓ᙮᙭᙮ᘔ

In a more important tiny bubble, Alene and I will do our best to raise Jannie to be everything she can be, Down syndrome be damned. After I hang them up, Alene's career will prosper and we'll do fine. We'll move to Vancouver, where most of her work is, and I'll spend a lot of time with Jannie. She'll be a sweet kid, but there are heart problems and a leg that needs straightening, creating an uncertain future for her and me both. My football past and all those helmet hits will come back to haunt me: foggy mornings will turn into long, dark days, and I'll worry about just how long I'll still be me.

I'll be in the dumps a lot, but I'll need something to do, someone to be, so I'll take care of Jannie, one day at a time. Today is today. There'll be speech therapy sessions and school and all the rest. There'll be some joy in this, some deep satisfaction. She'll be my girl, my always girl.

In this bubble, even as I lose some recent memories, I'll still remember certain moments from my past that were so perfect, where I was so tuned in—so fully one with the moment—that I captured them completely in my mind in slow-motion detail. I'll remember them vividly, even when I can't find my car keys. I will still feel the perfection of the pass to Elijah Depps deep in the corner of the end zone against the Argos. And I'll still watch in awe that time I swear I guided the ball in flight to bend it around Ryan Crisps' outstretched hands as he tried to intercept for the Blue Bombers, and instead the ball found Jason Wissen with no time left, and we won.

And I'll feel that joy, too, when Jannie, on her twenty-second birthday, in one of her many Special Olympics soccer games, steals the ball off the player she's defending and sprints down the field with it, dribbling like mad. She'll weave her way past three defenders, come in on the goalie, fake left and shoot right, an outside of the shoe push into the upper ninety for a goal. It'll be a great goal, and everybody on both teams will come over to hug her and celebrate, because that's how it's done in Special O's. I'll beam. That's my girl.

੦੩ ੩੶~੬ ੪੦

There's another tiny bubble, one I imagine every now and then, where after my divorce I'll spend a lot of time with a woman named Emily. She won't be bothered by Jannie; she'll just want me to be me, Jannie to be Jannie, and Emily to be Emily.

In that bubble we'll make it work. There'll be a new drug on the market for trisomy 21, and the sun will shine every day and the Yankees will never, *ever* win the pennant, but the Ticats will be the powerhouse team of the CFL and my knees won't hurt and my mind will be clear and I'll keep all my memories as Jannie goes off to college and the sun will shine every day in Hamilton, Ontario.

੦੩ ੩੶~੬ ੪੦

In one particular spot in one particular tiny bubble, Alene will be a grad student when we meet, and an associate professor by the time she leaves for a post in Quebec. She can't turn it down, and the stress and strain of raising Jannie, she'll say in distancing French, is *complètement impossible*. I'll have seen it coming for years, but we'll still do the divorce through lawyers.

As time goes by, she'll call Jannie often enough, and send her cards and cash on her birthday and Christmas. She'll even bring Jannie up for a week or two to visit in the summer.

Jannie will do fine. By her sixteenth birthday she'll be doing third-grade arithmetic and fourth-grade reading and tearing things up in Special Olympics soccer. This will be better than the school-district psychologist thought Jannie would ever do. It will be so good, in fact, that after her birthday party, after the neighbor kids and her special pals are gone, after the cake is eaten, she'll be sitting on her bed kicking a plastic toy soccer ball off the opposite wall: shoot it, trap it with her foot, shoot it again, trap it, shoot it, trap it.

I'll come in to stop the racket and she'll look at me: that wide face, those eyes. Her language skills aren't all that great, but from the look on her face I'll be able to see something's up. "My father," she'll say, "I sixteen now."

I'll sit down next to her. "Yeah, young lady. You're growing up fast," I'll say, but what I'll be thinking about is all the things Jannie I have learned together, often the hard way. Boyfriends, how to handle her periods, what clothes to wear and when to wear them, how to tie her hair in a ponytail and put in a different bow every day, how to ignore some people and pay attention to others, how to be so different and still be so happy. Tricky business, all of that.

"My father," she'll say, "I not be like you or Mom-mom."

I'll be the lunkhead I am in every one of these bubbles, no question, but I'll be able to see where this is going: my Jannie, my hard-working girl, is doing so well that she knows how well she isn't doing. She's been expecting to grow up, to leave Neverland. But in this bubble . . . it doesn't work like that.

"Jannie, Jannie," I'll say, lying to her and not for the first time, struggling with how to handle this. "Look," I'll say, "We're all different, Janster, we all have different things we're good at or bad at."

She'll look at me. She'll trust me. I'll say, "I wanted to be an astronomer, Jannie. You know, look at the stars and figure out what it all means. I wanted that, Jannie, in the worst way. But I couldn't do the math."

"Bet Mom could," Jannie will say, smiling, getting into it.

"Yeah, Jannie, your mom sure could. She's one smart lady," I'll say, though I'll be thinking about what I might have said about Jannie's mother just then. To be kind, she'll have missed out on a lot of good things.

"Sure, my father. I get it," Jannie will say. And then she'll stand up to give me a hug, and I'll hug her back and then I'll leave the room. Later, out in the driveway, we'll shoot hoops and she'll seem fine. I'll go out and join her in a game of one-on-one, make it-take it, and she'll clobber me. I'll blame it on my bad knees.

⋇⟡⟡⋇

In my least favorite bubble I'll die at age fifty-two of an aneurysm. Alene won't be around and I'll have no living relatives. I won't leave much money behind. Jannie will be stranded. Alone. Unhappy. And there'll be twenty more years of her own decline into senescence before there's peace.

CR ❧ ◦ᴥ◦ ℣

In another bubble, Jannie will be an intellectual powerhouse. In high school she'll think calculus is fun and physics is entertaining. She'll have a perfect score on the science portion of the PSAT. Caltech will come calling, and MIT, and Yale and Stanford and Loyola and Case Western and Harvey Mudd and Duke and the University of Chicago. Astronomy in college? Physics? Biology? She'll find it hard to decide.

She'll be patient with me in this bubble. She'll understand that her father is a decent guy, but not the sharpest tool in the shed. When she walks across the stage for that college degree, and then the next one, and then the next one, I'll there in the audience, proud as I can be.

CR ❧ ◦ᴥ◦ ℣

In one particular bubble, Jannie and I will be at the Brock Theatre in Hamilton, where we both live—me in a two-bedroom condo, Jannie in a group home that she's recently moved into after years of living in her own apartment. Down syndrome people slide into early-onset Alzheimer's, almost all of them. It's unfair, but there it is.

Jannie will be thirty years old and I'll be fifty-seven. We'll be laughing and joking about old age on that January day as we walk through the parking lot snow, go into the sudden warmth of the theater, buy our tickets, and take our seats. Then we'll watch a movie, something about memory keepers and cute Down syndrome kids and the sweet and soapy ills of the world. I'll be squirming in my seat; Jannie will be quiet.

When we walk out of the place people will be staring at Jannie. She'll not be cute, and she'll be shuffling some because of some knee trouble that I probably caused her, encouraging all that Special O's soccer and getting her out on the basketball court with me for all those years. We won't have played in a while.

It will be snowing lightly as we walk away from the theater and get in the car, a beat-up little Toyota that I'm determined to keep running.

You don't get rich in the CFL, and there are better uses for my retirement money than buying shiny new metal and plastic. As I start the car and get the heater going, Jannie will look at me. I'll see it in her eyes. That movie was a bad idea.

"My father," she'll say. "I. Am. Me." And she'll punch herself in the chest with her right fist, hard.

"You are that, Jannie, you certainly are," I'll say, kicking myself.

"Thank you," she'll say, and sit back and relax.

There are all those different bubbles, but right then and right there, this will be the only one that matters. This is it. Reality. We are who we are.

We are where we are in this bubble, the one we share, the one where we do the best we can with what we have.

We won't talk about the movie as we drive off and head for some ice cream, and then, later, the group home. Instead, we'll talk hockey, father and daughter, something about the Sabres and how maybe they'll move to Hamilton and wouldn't that be great? Or we'll talk about Jannie's bowling team, where she's holding down that ninety-six average and I couldn't possibly be more proud of her. Or we'll talk about the Ticats and how much fun we had going to the games last summer and fall and soon enough the season will be back and this year, for sure, the Ticats will make their way back to the Grey Cup.

We won't talk about the path I've started walking down. Jannie wouldn't understand. But the reason she's in that group home is that they don't trust me to have her anymore. Mood swings. Anger. All those hits in all those practices and all those games. CTE my doc calls it, and the league agrees. I have good days and bad ones, and she's safer in that home.

I'm not happy about that.

I was counting on holding Jannie's hand as she crossed that street into the confusion, and then the darkness she faces, and now it's her who'll be holding mine.

But that won't come up. We won't say much about anything. We won't need to. We'll just eat our ice cream and hang out together and enjoy this little bit of a bubble as best we can. This is our bubble, right here and right now.

Today is today.

ART BY CHRISTOPHER WOODS

Contributors

Creative Nonfiction

Devin Donovan lives in Charlottesville, VA where he teaches Writing & Critical Inquiry at the University of Virginia. His work has appeared in *The Windsor Review*, *Mantis*, *Black Heart Magazine* and elsewhere.

Christine Holmstrom still occasionally wonders why she took a job at San Quentin—the notorious men›s maximum security prison. Karma or cosmic accident? But after surviving riots, an armed escape and a death threat, she finally had the good sense to retire and is working on a memoir about her prison years.

Lee Kahrs is a graduating member of the Stonecoast July 2018 Class, serving as Class Rep and the CNF Graduation Speaker. She lives in Vermont, where she is the managing editor of *The Reporter* weekly newspaper in Brandon, circulation 1,500. This essay is one of fifteen in Lee's thesis, *Hair on Fire: Essays From a Life*. Her essay about her teen idol, Jennifer Beals, is included in the anthology of women writers, *Idol Talk: Women Writers on the Teenage Fascinations That Changed their Lives*, edited by Elizabeth Searle and Tamra Wilson. The essay is titled "What a Feeling." The anthology is being published by McFarland in July 2018.

Judith is retired, lives in Manhattan, and helps the economy by shopping for shoes much too often. She dotes on her two perfect grandchildren. She writes fiction and creative nonfiction, and tries her very best to tell the truth.

Dee Nathan is a screenwriter and is shooting a feature documentary. When not working, she spends an inordinate amount of time helping her adult children become more adult.

Jenny O'Connell's book project, *Finding Petronella*, traces her solo trek across Finland in the footsteps of a female Lappish gold legend. Her work has appeared in or is forthcoming from *Camas* and *Slice Magazine*, and was featured in the island art installation *Surface First Tilts West*. She earned her Master's in Creative Writing from Stonecoast MFA.

Bill O'Heaney hails from upstate New York. Bill has been a chef, a non-profit administrator, a stay-at-home dad, and a licensed professional mental health counselor. Bill lives with his wife and daughter in Connecticut and works as a school counselor.

Helen Waters is a writer, performer, and filmmaker. Her work has been published in *The Southampton Review*, *New York Tyrant*, and *Maura Magazine*. She can next be seen as the lead in the interactive web pilot "What's Good." She has several feature films in development. She was born and raised in Bastrop County, Texas, and she lives and works in Brooklyn, New York.

Fiction

C.R. Beideman writes from Bozeman, Montana. His fiction appears or is forthcoming in *Yellow Medicine Review* and the anthologies *Awake in the World* by Riverfeet Press, *Triangulation: Appetites by Parsec*, *Ink and This Side of the Divide* by Baobab Press in conjunction with the University of Nevada.

Carina Bissett is a writer, poet, and educator working primarily in the fields of speculative fiction and interstitial art. Her short fiction and poetry has been published in multiple journals and anthologies including *Hath No Fury, Gorgon: Stories of Emergence, Mythic Delirium, NonBinary Review,* and *Timeless Tales.* Her work has been nominated for several awards and she was the recipient of the 2016 HWA Scholarship.

Theodora Goss is the World Fantasy Award-winning author of the short story collection *In the Forest of Forgetting* (2006); *Interfictions* (2007), a short story anthology coedited with Delia Sherman; *Voices from Fairyland* (2008), a poetry anthology with critical essays and a selection of her own poems; *The Thorn and the Blossom* (2012), a novella in a two-sided accordion format; the poetry collection *Songs for Ophelia* (2014); debut novel *The Strange Case of the Alchemist's Daughter* (2017); and sequel *European Travel for the Monstrous Gentlewoman* (2018). She has been a finalist for the Nebula, Locus, Crawford, Seiun, and Mythopoeic Awards, as well as on the Tiptree Award Honor List. Her work has been translated into twelve languages. She teaches literature and writing at Boston University and in the Stonecoast MFA Program. Visit her at theodoragoss.com.

Jennifer Falkner's short stories have appeared in *The Jellyfish Review, THEMA* and *LitroNY*, among other places. Recently she won the *Firewords Quarterly* Writing Competition. She lives in Ottawa, Canada.

Alyssa Hamilton is a writer based in New England. She is a student of the Etowah Valley MFA program at Reinhardt University. Previous work has appeared in *Halo Literary Magazine, The Blue Mountain Review,* and *Wyvern Lit.*

Kaely Horton is a second-year MFA candidate at the University of New Hampshire and the fiction editor of *Barnstorm Journal*. Her work has appeared in *Smokelong Quarterly, RipRap Literary Journal, Gravel,* and *Flash Fiction Online*. She resides on the Oregon Coast.

James Van Pelt teaches high school English in western Colorado part time and writes the rest of the time. His fiction has made numerous appearances in most of the major science fiction and fantasy magazines. He has been a finalist for a Nebula Award, the Sturgeon Award, the Colorado Blue Spruce Young Adult Book Award, and been reprinted in many year's best collections. His first novel, *Summer of the Apocalypse,* was released in 2006 and was named a Best Book for Young Adults by the American Library Association. His third collection of stories, *The Radio Magician and Other Stories,* received the Colorado Book Award in 2010. His latest collection, *The Experience Arcade and Other Stories* debuted at the World Fantasy Convention last year. He blogs at http://jamesvanpelt.com.

Alexander Weinstein is the Director of The Martha's Vineyard Institute of Creative Writing and the author of the collection *Children of the New World.* He lives in Ann Arbor, Michigan.

Rick Wilber is a visiting assistant professor of creative writing in the low-residency MFA program at Western State Colorado University. He is the editor of several anthologies, has published some fifty short stories, several novels and short-story collections, and a handful of college textbooks on writing and mass-media studies. He lives in Florida, where he often plays basketball with his Down syndrome son.

Poetry

Carrie Carrie is a reader and writer based in Bournemouth, England. She has a BA in Creative Writing and Philosophy and an MA in English Literature. She is fond of punctuation as passing-of-time and iambic pentameter, and interested in how poems are simultaneously the same and different when read silently and read non-silently. She primarily writes about things/non-things she finds beautiful and things/non-things she finds interesting (which are sometimes the same things/non-things). Her favorite poet is Oscar Wilde and her favorite lyricist is John Darnielle.

Liz N. Clift loves opportunities to explore the world—in travel, but especially in her communities, because she believes there's such depth of beauty even in the mundane, when we give ourselves permission to settle into ourselves. Her poetry has previously appeared in *Stonecoast Review* as well as *Rattle, Passages North, The National Poetry Review,* and elsewhere.

Genevieve DeGuzman was born in the Philippines, raised in Southern California, and graduated from Columbia University. Her poetry appears in *Alluvian, Connotation Press: An Online Artifact, FIVE:2:ONE, Flyway, FOLIO, Liminality, LONTAR, Reed Magazine, Strange Horizons, Switchback,* and *Thin Air.* She was a finalist for the 2018 Atticus Review Winter Poetry Contest, the 2018 Sonia Sanchez-Langston Hughes Poetry Prize, and the 2017 Lauren K. Alleyne Difficult Fruit Poetry Prize. She has been a literary arts resident at Can Serrat and lives in Portland, Oregon. Find her online at: about.me/genevievedeguzman.

Oonagh C. Doherty was born in Scotland, and grew up in both the United Kingdom and the United States, but immersion in the pan-latino cultures of the Spanish Americans, including the U.S.A., has also been an influence. She has published poetry and prose in many venues. Her book, *During the Truce*, a memoir of Bogota, Colombia, during the turbulent 1980s was published in October 2015. You can find more information at her website, https://oonaghcdoherty.weebly.com.

Ann Howells, of Dallas, Texas, edited *Illya's Honey* eighteen years, recently digitally at www.IllyasHoney.com. Her books include: *Under a Lone Star* (Village Books Press, 2016) and an anthology of D/FW poets which she edited, *Cattlemen & Cadillacs* (Dallas Poets Community Press, 2016). Her chapbook, *Softly Beating Wings* (Blackbead Books, 2017), was published as winner of the William D. Barney Chapbook Contest. Her work appears in many small press and university publications.

Laurie Kolp's poems have appeared in *Stirring*, *Whale Road Review*, *Rust + Moth*, and more. Her poetry books include the full-length *Upon the Blue Couch* and chapbook *Hello, It's Your Mother*. Laurie lives in southeast Texas with her husband, three children, and two dogs.

Roselyn Kubek would like to be an enigma, but appears to be just what she is: a former English Department Chair, a current tutor and teacher supervisor, and a writer and lover of poetry. Her work has appeared in several journals including, most recently, *The Avocet*, *The Leaflet*, and *Pink Panther Magazine*. She was twice an NEATE Poet of the Year finalist. Roz lives in Pembroke, Massachusetts, and weekends in Raymond, Maine, with her husband and dog.

Madeline Miele was raised on the coast of Maine and feels most at home by the ocean. She is living in New York and working on her first collection of poems.

Orlan is a Stonecoast alumnus who graduated with an emphasis in poetry December 2016.

Melinda Thomsen's chapbooks *Naming Rights* and *Field Rations* are from Finishing Line Press. Her poems have appeared in *Tar River Poetry*, *The Comstock Review*, *Poetry East*, *New York Quarterly*, *Rattle* and anthologies such as *The Bug Book, Heart of the Order,* and *Token Entry*. She lives in Greenville, North Carolina, and teaches composition at Pitt Community College.

After graduating from Southeastern Oklahoma State in 2010, **Travis Truax** spent several years working in various national parks out west, including Zion, Olympic and Yellowstone. His work has appeared or is forthcoming in *Quarterly West*, *Gravel*, *Bird's Thumb*, *The Pinch*, *Raleigh Review* and *The Cossack Review*. He is in Bozeman, Montana.

Candelin Wahl is a Vermont writer whose work can be found in *Red Wolf Journal, MockingHeart Review, Tuck Magazine, HerStory* and other journals. She is Poetry Co-Editor of *Mud Season Review*. Of this poem, she says, "It surprised me that despite bearing two healthy daughters after the miscarriage, more than thirty years ago, that loss was so palpable." Website: candelinwahl.com   Twitter: @beachdreamvt

Sarah Broussard Weaver is an MFA candidate at the Rainier Writing Workshop. Her work has appeared in *Lunch Ticket, Full Grown People, The Nervous Breakdown*, and *Hippocampus*, among others. She lives with her family in the hills of Portland, Oregon.

Abigail Warren's poetry has appeared in over twenty literary magazines. She has a new book of poetry available, *Air-Breathing Life* from Finishing Line Press, 2017.

Dramatic Works

Rita Anderson, a member of Poets & Writers, Academy of American Poets, has an MFA Poetry and an MA Playwriting. Poetry editor at the University of New Orleans, Rita has two volumes of poetry published: *Watched Pots (A Lovesong to Motherhood)*, and *The Entropy of Rocketman* (Finishing Line Press). Rita won the Houston Poetry Festival, the Gerreighty Prize, the Robert F. Gibbons Poetry Award, the Cheyney Award, and an award from the Academy of American Poets. Her poems have appeared in almost 100 literary journals and anthologies including *Spoon River Poetry Review, EVENT Magazine, Waves (AROHO), Old Northwest Review, Blue Heron Review, Ellipsis, The Longleaf Pine, Cahoodaloodaling, The Blueshift Journal, Blotterature, Words Work, Transcendence, PHIction, Persona* (50th Anniversary Edition), *The Artful Mind, Our Write Side, Di-Verse-City: An Austin Poetry Anthology, Inflight Magazine, The Stardust Gazette*, and *Explorations* (University of Alaska Press). Rita is Senior Poetry Editor for Red Dashboard Publishing, and she lives in Austin. Contact Rita at www.rita-anderson.com.

Art

Jeffrey Alfier's recent books include *Fugue for a Desert Mountain, Anthem for Pacific Avenue* and *The Red Stag at Carrbridge: Scotland Poems*. Recent credits include *Copper Nickel, Meridian, Midwest Quarterly, Poetry Ireland Review*, and *The McNeese Review*. He is founder and co-editor of Blue Horse Press.

Giuseppe Donatiello was born in 1967 and lives in Oria (Puglia) in southern Italy. He has been a professional radio host since 1979 and is a scientific journalist. For the astronomical monthly magazine Nuovo Orione (in the past also for other national magazines), he writes columns related to news on the amateur instrumentation for astronomy, testing of new instruments, advanced image processing techniques, and history of astronomy (specifically medieval in the Mediterranean Basin). Because of these activities, he has the opportunity to use telescopes and astro-cameras of various kinds. He does not have a private observatory, but a semi-fixed station where instruments are stationed. He builds his own optics (an apochromatic refractor ED 127mm f/9) and astro-cameras. In the mid-nineties he was one of the first in Italy to build a cooled CCD (disused) and one of the first, in 2010, to experience the potential of cooled CMOS sensors, especially in near-infrared (NIR). With these cold CMOS, he has developed capturing techniques using short exposures, lucky imaging, and even deep-sky as his main interest. As an amateur astronomer, he participated (from 1985 to 1997) in the International Halley Watch (IHW) and the Ulysses Comet Watch (UCW). He seems to be the first to have documented the movement of Sirius B (with references), and also to have captured Procyon B with lucky imaging techniques. Very interested in galaxies and their evolution, he deals with research of dwarf galaxies and galactic archeology in which he can apply processing techniques to highlight weak structures and stellar streams. As a result of such research, he discovered a nearby dwarf galaxy (in publication). He has about 1,200 publications in magazines and websites.

Carl Erickson is a volunteer firefighter living in Buckley, Washington.

Maria Green: There is beauty all around us, we just need to open our hearts to see it. Along the way I love to capture these beautiful moments.

Jim Ross resumed creative pursuits in 2015 after retiring from public health research. He's since published seventy pieces of nonfiction, several poems, and 180 photos in seventy-five journals in North America, Europe, and Asia, such as *Bombay Gin, Columbia Journal, Ilanot Review, Lunch Ticket, MAKE*, and *The Atlantic*. He and his wife normally split their time between Maryland and West Virginia, but love to travel too. Jim's ideal is to tell nonfiction stories supported by images that beckon readers to return.

David B. Such is a left-handed mechanical engineer with nearly four decades of experience with turbines and other machinery. Off the job, he retreats to his home in the foothills of Colorado where contrasted to his industrial work environment, he appreciates close connections with his natural surroundings and enjoys reading, writing, drawing, and gardening. David enjoys sketching with a loose, free-form style as a way to counterbalance the precision demanded by his day job working with turbomachinery. His creative work (essays, poetry, and drawings) has appeared in *The Flaneur* and *South 85 Literary Journal* and is forthcoming in *Weber – The Contemporary West, The Doctor T.J. Eckleburg Review*, and *Korean Quarterly*. Visit David at dbsuch.wordpress.com and dbsuchart.wordpress.com.

Brett Stout is a 38-year-old writer and artist originally from Atlanta, Georgia. He is a high school dropout and former construction worker turned college graduate and paramedic. He writes now while mainly hung-over on white lined paper in a small cramped apartment in Myrtle Beach, SC. He has published several novels of prose and poetry including *Lab Rat Manifesto*, and has been featured in a vast range of various media including the University of California and *Litro Magazine UK*.

Travis Volk is a film and digital photographer and elementary teacher based in southwest Washington. He explores the ethos of different regions by capturing portraits, found items and architecture. He captures the unexpected beauty in the ordinary and what is often looked over. View more of his work on Instagram @tvolkphotography.

Russell Wilson is a TV news journalist in Portland, Maine, and is in his second semester at Stonecoast. In previous lives he has been a middle school teacher, football coach, ski bum, and summer camp counselor from Texas to Oregon to South Dakota to New England. He tends to write YA fiction and always chooses a window seat when he flies.

Christopher Woods is a writer, teacher and photographer who lives in Chappell Hill, Texas. His photographs can be seen in his gallery -http://christopherwoods.zenfolio.com.